Judith Jack~~on~~ ~~w~~riter specialis~~t~~ ~~with the motor~~ industry. ~~Sh~~ ~~motoring~~ the *Guardian*, presenter of BBC te~~levision~~ and *Roadworthy* series, and a regu~~lar~~ *Homes and Gardens*. She is marrie~~d~~

606

every woman's guide to the car

JUDITH JACKSON

Published by VIRAGO PRESS Limited 1993
20–23 Mandela Street, Camden Town, London NW1 0HQ

Copyright © Judith Jackson 1993

The right of Judith Jackson to be identified as Author of this work
has been asserted by her in accordance with the Copyright,
Designs and Patents Act 1988.

*A CIP catalogue record for this book is available from the British
Library*

Printed in Great Britain by Cox & Wyman Ltd, Reading, Berkshire

Typeset by Goodfellow & Egan Ltd, Cambridge

Contents

Acknowledgements

I am indebted to many friends, relations and colleagues in the motor industry for their help in the preparation of this book – particularly Maggie Rowlands of the Automobile Association, Liz Pelling of Ford of Europe, Amanda Gadeselli of Nissan, Gordon Sked of Rover, Laura Warren of Volkswagen (UK), Elizabeth Aves of Avenue Communications, and Jeff Daniels whose patience at unsociable hours is beyond price.

JJ

Introduction

It is now nearly a hundred years since Bertha Benz, a German wife and mother, borrowed her husband's newly developed and revolutionary vehicle to take their sons on a sixty-two mile trip from Mannheim to Pforzheim, thus completing the world's first long distance trip in a motor car.

Despite that auspicious start, motoring was to remain a predominantly male preserve for several decades. It took two world wars – when women were needed to drive ambulances, build engines, service and maintain vehicles – for women drivers to break the male automotive domination. Once women discovered how liberating a car can be, they have continued to drive into freedom.

More than fourteen million women in Britain have a driving licence, accounting for nearly half the drivers on the road – and the figure grows daily. More than a third of women motorists buy and pay for their own car. Increasingly, car manufacturers are waking up to this fact and looking at the needs of women when designing and engineering cars. And women are now to be found working in car plants, dealerships, garages and showrooms.

But why a car book for women? Because there are two very real aspects that affect the woman driver in a way that makes her enjoyment and use of a car quite different than a man. One is the stereotype of the 'lady driver' – dizzy, feckless, incompetent, who doesn't know the bonnet from the boot – a deeply undermining image. Maybe as a result, cars tend to be looked upon as great metal mysteries (by many men too). This book presents straightforward information in a straight-talking form, which tells women everything they need to know about the everyday business of motoring and the motor car.

The other aspect that largely affects women is the more serious issue of safety. Sadly, because of some tragic incidents, relatively few, but dreadful nevertheless, women have been made to feel vulnerable on the road. And this vulnerability is exacerbated by the media and by advertisers. What I have done is to explain how, with understanding, preparation and commonsense, a women can be as safe on the road as a man – and still enjoy her motoring.

Finally, this book is about running a car responsibly in a country dramatically affected by overcrowded roads and automobile pollution.

The opportunity and ability to drive a car gives women an independence and mobility which our grandmothers never dreamed of. *Every Woman's Guide to the Car* is for the millions of women – young, old, learners and experienced – in the driving seat today.

Judith Jackson, 1993

The Good Driver

▶ KEEPS THE CAR IN GOOD CONDITION

▶ ALWAYS WEARS A SEAT BELT

▶ ANTICIPATES TRAFFIC, THE ROAD AND THE
UNEXPECTED

▶ ALWAYS CONCENTRATES

▶ IS CONSIDERATE OF OTHER ROAD USERS

▶ DOES NOT DRINK AND DRIVE

▶ PLANS JOURNEYS AHEAD

▶ MAKES SURE PASSENGERS ARE
COMFORTABLE AND SAFE

▶ READS THIS BOOK

1. Buying a Car

Owning a car can be exciting and liberating. But it is expensive. Although buying a car was once a uniquely male preserve, more and more women are now not only choosing a car but paying for it themselves. But before you part with your money, there are some crucial points to consider.

WHY BUY A CAR?

There may be dozens of excuses for buying a car, but there is only one good reason in these days of traffic congestion – that you cannot manage without one. However, even if you are fortunate enough to be able to buy a car when you don't really need one, you should still consider the cost not only to yourself but to the environment, as well as the headaches it will undoubtedly cause. A car should never be an impulse purchase.

COST

It is well known that a car is the second most expensive purchase any of us is likely to make – the first being a home. But what is less well understood is that the cost of running a car is considerable. The average annual cost of owning and running a car is approximately £3,500. This figure (calculated by the AA from data in the 1990 *Family Expenditure Survey*) includes depreciation, interest on a loan or hire purchase, service and maintenance, insurance, parking and fuel, but does not take into consideration any fines you may pick up along the way. In 1993 the figure is higher, with escalating insurance premiums, fluctuating fuel prices and increasing depreciation as the second-hand car market suffers recession.

BUYING A NEW CAR

If you can afford the initial outlay (which can be anywhere between approximately £4,250 and £165,000) a new car has the obvious advantage of its pristine condition. It should be totally reliable but in case it isn't, it comes with the **manufacturer's warranty**. Warranties are becoming more valuable all the time – some are for up to six years and most now cover corrosion as well as mechanical failure.

The cost of servicing and maintaining a brand-new car will almost certainly be lower than that for a second-hand vehicle, and because it benefits from the latest technology, a new model will comply with all the latest safety regulations, be more fuel efficient and less polluting than an older car.

Although raising the money for a second-hand car may be difficult, a new car depreciates more quickly (about 18 per cent when the number plates are fitted and before the car turns a wheel) so you will not get your money back if you are forced to sell the car while it is relatively new.

BUYING SECOND-HAND

Many people with financial restraints opt for second-hand cars, but unless you are a useful car mechanic and able to take care of the car yourself, a second-hand car, which costs you less to buy, could end up by costing you more. This is less likely if you are buying a 'nearly new' car from a reputable dealer, but in any case it is worth finding someone who knows a bit about cars to go with you when you are choosing one.

Reliability is the most important quality in a car (there is no point in having a car that doesn't start), so a lot of time and money can be taken up in keeping an old car on the road.

If you have to borrow money to buy a car, you will find that your bank manager is less likely to accommodate you if you tell him that your heart is set on a 1987 Alfa Romeo than if you claim allegiance to a brand new Ford Fiesta. Be realistic.

Before you go shopping for a car, analyse your motoring habits:

▶ How many people will you be carrying?
▶ Are most of your passengers young or old?
▶ Do you regularly carry large loads?
▶ Will the car be garaged?
▶ How many miles do you drive during a year?

WHAT TYPES OF CAR ARE AVAILABLE?
Saloon cars

Saloon cars ('notch-backs') have two or four-side doors and a conventional boot which may lock independently but which has limitations of size.

Hatchbacks

These have either two or four-side doors plus a sloping rear tailgate which opens from bumper to roof, giving access to the luggage space. Hatchbacks usually have rear seats that fold down, either completely or in part, to give more load space. A hatchback has the versatility of height in the luggage space, but unless you cover it, the world can inspect your cargo.

Estate cars (once called 'station wagons')

Estate cars are designed for large or cumbersome loads. They may have two or four-side doors, and have a squared-off rear end with a high-opening tailgate. The estate car also has a beefier suspension to cope with the extra weight that it is expected to carry. Some large estate cars also have a third row of seats, facing forwards or backwards.

Convertibles

Convertibles have soft hoods which fold back either by hand or automatically, and usually only two seats in the front with two (very) occasional seats behind. Although modern hoods are remarkably robust, they are also very tempting to people with sharp implements, cats with sharp claws, and birds. So, unless you can garage your car when you are not using it, a convertible is not a sensible buy.

Multi-purpose vehicles (MPVS)

These come in a variety of shapes and sizes, but all are tall and capacious. Some have sliding doors like vans, and some have several seating options, which you can change at will.

The saloon or hatchback are the most popular cars. Although children should *always* be in a safety seat or wear a seat belt, accidents can happen and it is reassuring to drive a car with only two-side doors, so that there is no danger of a door flying open by mistake and a child falling out. Elderly people, however, often find it difficult to climb behind the front seats of a two-side door into the back, so a four-side door version would be more practical. Estate cars should act as workhorses, and carry heavy loads, although some of the upmarket ones rarely seem to carry anything more demanding than the weekly shopping.

If a two-seater coupé is your dream because of its stylishness and performance, consider carefully how you will use it. Alone in the car, you will put handbag, briefcase or shopping on the passenger seat where they are easy targets for traffic-light thieves. And if you carry a passenger, you may find that cars with no space behind the seats and a tiny boot are inadequate, even for a weekend in the country.

THE CAR HIRE OPTION

There is no point in buying a car bigger than you will need simply because once a year you will need to tow a boat or take several friends on holiday for a fortnight. It makes much more financial sense to buy the vehicle which suits you for forty-eight weeks in the year, and hire one for holidays or special occasions. In fact drivers in Paris, whose parking problems make London look like a wide-open space, regularly hire cars for their motoring needs rather than buying one, avoiding the need for a permanent parking space as well as twelve-month tax and insurance.

ENGINE SIZE

Engine size does not refer to the dimensions of the engine, but to its cubic capacity – for example 1600c.c. or 1.6 litres. The higher the cubic capacity, the higher the performance and fuel consumption and, as a result, the insurance premium. Most family cars have engines between 950c.c. and 2500c.c., but just to confuse you, a smaller engine fitted with a turbo-charger (see Glossary) will come into the high-performance category. There are no hard and fast rules about engines, but generally speaking small engines are great for short journeys around towns; if you do a lot of motorway mileage, a bigger engine will be better. If fuel costs are of prime importance to you, consider a diesel engine. Some cost more than the equivalent petrol engine and they do not always have the same sprightly acceleration, but for fuel economy they are unbeatable.

ANALYSE YOUR MOTORING NEEDS

Before you walk into a showroom or answer an advertisement, write down exactly what sort of car you want and what you can afford to pay, *and stick to it*. Only too often buyers set off with the best intentions but are persuaded to buy something unsuitable or too expensive.

Also decide in advance what equipment you need. There is a huge variation in standard equipment, so make a list of what you must have. **Power-assisted steering, central locking** and an **anti-lock braking system** (ABS) should be top of the shopping list if you can afford them (see Glossary). A good **alarm/anti-theft system** is almost mandatory in urban areas these days, but most sunshine roofs are of limited use. If you travel long distances, a good **radio/cassette player** is a welcome companion, but most important of all for the high-mileage driver is a **comfortable seat.** *Never, never, never* buy a car until you are completely satisfied that the seat is the right one for you – one that is inadequate will not only cause discomfort, but will also substantially contribute to any back problems you may be susceptible to.

A motoring magazine that carries a complete list of the models available and current new car prices (*Autocar* and *Buying Cars* are good for this) is invaluable at this stage. But prices are not carved in tablets of stone, and there is usually room for negotiation. Beware of being negotiated above your budget limit, or into buying the wrong car. You probably only buy a car every few years and lack experience, whereas the person selling you a car is a professional whose job depends on selling a car a week. Faced with a persuasive salesman, it can sometimes be difficult to stick to your guns. Never be afraid to walk away.

Your equipment list will ensure that you do not forget an essential item, and may provide a useful basis for price negotiation. Before you agree to any purchase, get the salesman to write down what *the total price* of the car will be – including delivery, number plates, a tank of fuel and any other extras the dealer is likely to dream up. This figure, not the basic price of the car, is the one you should budget for.

WHAT MAKE OF CAR TO BUY

Having decided on the type and specification of the car you need, you will be faced with a choice of makes. There is no longer a simple answer to this. Once upon a time one could say with certainty that the Xmobile was a better buy than the Ymobile, and that the Zmobile should be avoided at all costs. Improvements throughout the industry mean that this is no longer possible (or wise, if litigation is to be avoided). Although Skoda and Lada jokes are still bandied around, even these makes have improved out of all recognition in the past five years. Construction and use regulations do not allow a seriously unsafe new car to be offered for sale and the competitive market ensures that quality and reliability standards are relatively uniform. For as many makes of car as there are on sale, you will find someone to claim that the Amobile is either the best or worst car on the road. A new current car from a recognised manufacturer is a good start.

Try to buy a car from a local dealer. If the nearest dealer – and therefore source of servicing and spares – is a long way from your home you will be seriously inconvenienced when the car needs attention.

Some dealers are better than others. Word of mouth is usually the best source of information about this. A local dealer will be very concerned about his or her reputation and should be eager to treat you well, whereas the dealer a hundred miles away will be less concerned that you will criticise him in public.

If you are tempted to buy one of the more exotic makes, or an older model, bear in mind that it will need frequent and probably expensive service and maintenance. Not everybody will be eager to carry this out, so a good relationship with a local garage can be worth its weight in gold.

You can buy from:

- a car showroom
- a second-hand car dealer
- a car auction
- newspapers or magazines
  privately

There are several ways of buying a car. You can go to your local dealer, who will sell new cars and may have second-hand cars in stock. Or you can go to a second-hand car dealer. You can reply to advertisements in the press, you can go to an auction, or you can buy from a friend. If you have never bought a car before, it can be a daunting process. Reasonable precautions will reduce the risks to a minimum and if you have the luxury of a knowledgeable friend, he or she can be a great asset.

If you have never bought a car before, and know little about them, it is unquestionably safer to buy a new car from a reputable dealer. If a manufacturer entrusts its franchise to a dealer, then you can be assured of certain standards – and if something goes wrong you have someone to complain to. Many franchised dealers also sell second-hand cars, and the same rules apply to these.

Although the market recognises the rapidly growing numbers of female buyers, sadly there are still dealers who regard a solo woman customer as insignificant. If you encounter this type of dealer and have a choice, go somewhere else, but try and find time to write a stern note to the managing directors of both the dealership and the manufacturer, complaining. Only then will things improve. If you go to a dealer with no franchise, and who only sells second-hand cars, you will need to know what you are looking for as well as what you are being offered.

However you buy a car, whether new or second-hand, it is essential to test-drive it. Ten miles is an absolute minimum, and sitting next to the salesman is not good enough.

The AA and RAC offer an inspection service for members. For a fee – approximately £100 – they will inspect and report on a second-hand car, or even a new one if you feel it necessary.

Reputable dealers will have no objection to this, although if the car you are interested in is genuinely popular, the dealer may try to persuade you to make up your mind immediately.

Never allow yourself to be hurried into making a decision on a car purchase. There are endless numbers of cars on the market and if you cannot buy this one, there are sure to be others as good, if not better, just down the road. Don't feel guilty about walking away.

Part-exchanges

If you have a car to part-exchange, get a good idea of what it is worth before you start to negotiate seriously. Because part-exchange values vary enormously, take a straw poll of local dealers, asking what they would offer in part-exchange against the sort of car you are interested in buying, and take an average.

If you have a part-exchange you will probably not get as good a deal as if you offer cash, but you will be saved the hassle and the expense of trying to sell your old car privately. And if you ask for a valuation and then wait six weeks before going back to strike a deal, the figure may well have changed. The car market is volatile and prices fluctuate for all sorts of reasons ranging from new model launches, interest rates and fuel prices to adverse publicity and the weather.

Advertisements

The same rules apply, only more so. A car that appears to be advertised privately is perhaps being sold by a dealer trading from a private address. Check that the name on the registration document ('log book') is that of the person selling the car, and if the registration document is not available, walk away. Again, insist on an AA or RAC inspection. A genuinely private seller will not be interested in a part-exchange or hire purchase, but will negotiate for cash.

Never go alone to see a car, particularly at night. Nor should you test-drive a car with a complete stranger, perhaps in an unfamiliar area. Take a couple of friends with you.

Car auctions

The world of the car auction is a very professional one and unless you know exactly what you are doing, it is best avoided. There is jargon which you need to understand, and it is hard not to feel intimidated. If you are determined to buy or sell a car at auction (or want a fascinating experience) go to one which is a member of

SMA (Society of Motor Auctions). Spend at least one session at an auction before you take part and never buy a car 'as seen', which means that you will have no redress if the car is faulty. If there is a car auction in your area, you will find it in the Yellow Pages.

> The first filmed commercial in Britain featuring a woman as motorist was made in 1938 by Ford and presented by Ursula Bloom. She recalls that proposals of marriage were frequently made by young men in cars which they had borrowed from their fathers. 'We now know that a woman is perfectly capable of handling a proposal of marriage, and her own car.'

PAPERWORK

Anyone selling a second-hand car should be able to provide you with all the relevant documents. You must insist on seeing the registration document (see Glossary), and ideally a purchase invoice which will prove that the person selling actually owns the car. If the car is more than three years old it should have a current Ministry of Transport (MoT) test certificate, which authenticates the state of the car *on the date it was tested*. There should also be a service history. Every new car comes with a service book, which should be stamped every time the car is serviced, and a careful owner will have kept all the bills for service and repairs, including tyres. These are a good guide to the genuine mileage of a car. As an extremely rough guide, the average private car does between 10,000 and 14,000 miles a year. Although it is illegal to 'clock' a car (turn the mileage indicator back so that the car appears to have done a low mileage), it still happens. The registration document carries the names of previous owners, if any, and if you have any doubts about the number of miles it is being claimed the car has done, it is quite acceptable to get in touch with them and ask for the mileage when they sold the car.

HOW TO PAY FOR THE CAR

There are various forms of finance for buying a car – cash; loans from banks or building societies; hire purchase; overdrafts; and schemes offered by manufacturers. Ask yourself these questions:

▶ Can you afford to pay cash?
▶ Is your bank helpful?
▶ How much will borrowing the money cost you?
▶ Can you afford the running costs? (These will be at least £115 a
   month if you have bought the car with cash – more if you have
   to pay interest on a loan or hire purchase.)

When it comes to buying a car, if you can manage it, cash (or a
cheque) reigns supreme. Not only will you be able to negotiate
with the dealer, who should be generous on discount in the face of
current adversity, but you will be spared interest rates. From time
to time manufacturers offer very attractive 'zero interest' deals, if
you can put up a substantial cash sum and pay the remainder off
quickly. If you pay by cheque, you will have to wait until the
cheque is cleared before the dealer will let you drive the car away.
In some cases this will take up to ten days, but the dealer can present your cheque to the bank for 'special clearance', for which
there will be a charge.

If you can negotiate a loan with your bank or building society,
then you can still haggle with the dealer on cash terms. But find
out how much the loan will cost you. What you need to know if
you borrow money, is the APR (annual percentage rate), which
will help you to assess how much the car will *really* cost you. A
bank or building society is unlikely to offer you an overdraft for
buying a car, but may be prepared to make a personal loan at a
fixed rate of interest.

If you take out a hire-purchase agreement, possibly offered to
you by the dealer, it is essential to know the APR and exactly how
much you will be paying during the time of the agreement. Don't
forget to add on the costs of running the car.

Almost all cars represent negative equity – i.e. they will never be
worth as much as you paid for them. *Cars are not an investment.*

KNOWING YOUR RIGHTS

There is a morass of consumer legislation on the subjects of buying
or selling cars, which you may have to struggle through if something goes wrong. If you buy a new car from a franchised dealer,
and pay the full list price on hire purchase with no part-exchange,
you will have the benefit of all the legislation available. But not
everyone does that, particularly in these days of haggling and barter.

If your new car develops faults, your first call must be to the dealer who sold it to you. It is sad but true that there are still many salesmen who regard female customers as ignorant and easily fobbed off. In every transaction, make a note of the person to whom you have spoken, either on the telephone or in person.

Make an appointment and take the car back to the dealer. Be prepared to spend some time explaining or demonstrating the faults, and leave the car at the dealership, explaining very clearly that you will not collect the car until it is in a condition suitable for the managing director's wife or partner to drive. A very few dealerships employ women in the sales department or as service receptionists, but these are few and far between. If you are fortunate enough to encounter either, it will help to encourage the trend if you ask to deal with them.

If you have a problem, give the dealer a chance to sort it out. If the fault occurs again, you need to go a stage further. Find out the name of the managing director (an anonymous call to the switchboard usually elicits this), and write a strong letter explaining the problem and asking for him/her to arrange for it to be fixed. Make sure that they know you are a woman who owns her own car. There is a distressing tendency for people to assume that every woman driver has a man with a chequebook behind her, but a percipient dealer will know that a woman customer who is treated correctly will pass the information on to friends and colleagues.

You should then get a phone call or letter asking for the car to be brought back. Write down, and keep, a summary of the problem as well as all the correspondence you receive. Do not let the process drag on for more than a few days.

If the problem is still not cured, your next recourse is to the manufacturer. A letter to the chairman, managing director or chief executive, sent by recorded delivery and copied to the managing director of the dealership, should be short and to the point. Name everyone you have had contact with, and don't be afraid to complain if you feel that you have been treated badly. It is important to remember that you have spent a lot of money and are entitled to be treated properly.

Every car, whether new or second-hand, is covered by the Sale of Goods and Misrepresentation Act, which means that the seller should describe it accurately. New cars also have to be of 'merchantable quality' – a vague phrase dreamt up by lawyers. So if your new car develops a fault in its early days, you must make a fuss immediately.

Making a fuss is a very time-consuming business. But unless the senior management of a manufacturer knows that it is selling substandard cars, it will never make improvements.

The AA, RAC and the Consumers' Association offer members legal advice on whether a complaint is reasonable, and how to proceed with it. As a last resort, the SMMT (Society of Motor Manufacturers and Traders) offers an arbitration service.

Second-hand cars

If you bought your car privately or at an auction, you have little or no chance of getting any money back. A second-hand car bought from a reputable dealer is subject to the same laws as new cars. The local Trading Standards Office may be able to help, if you think a law has been broken.

2. The Handbook

Have you got the handbook for your car?
Have you read it?

Apart from the Bible, the car handbook is the most widely distributed and least read book in the civilised world. If car owners realised how much trouble could be saved if they studied the handbook that comes with their car, it would be read avidly. Every car has a handbook when it is first sold but many never emerge from their plastic envelope. Handbooks may not be great literature but they provide the key to getting to grips with your car. If you know your handbook, you will understand your car and be much more confident in talking about it when you need help.

The handbook tells you all you need to know about the way your car works. Whether you buy a car new or second-hand, make sure it has a handbook. In the case of a second-hand car, make sure that the handbook you are given with the car relates to the car. Sometimes any old handbook finds its way into the glove compartment.

It is really advisable to spend half an hour or so studying the handbook. It is best to do this in the car so that you can work out how the controls work, as well as what the lights and graphics mean. Very importantly, it will show where reverse gear is. *Never* set off in an unfamiliar car without checking how to engage reverse gear. Find out how the seats can be adjusted so that you can sit comfortably, and how the door locks work. Today's cars are very sophisticated so there may be useful features on your car which you didn't expect.

The section concerned with regular car and maintenance probably includes diagrams. It is worth raising the bonnet and, even if you don't touch anything, identifying the parts shown in the handbook.

Keep the handbook in the glove compartment alongside a working torch so that you can read the handbook if you break down in the dark.

> 'I think she's a beauty but I wouldn't call her dear'
>
> Awful puns such as this figured in an advertisement for the 4/44 Wolseley in the 1950s. The car became 'she' early in her career about 1910, when only men bought cars and 'she' was faithful, if demanding. Although the habit has persisted, today it is only those men who lavish love and attention on their cars, who call them 'she'. Women tend to refer to their cars as 'it'.

WHAT HAPPENS IF YOU HAVE NO HANDBOOK?

If you have no handbook for your car, get one from the manufacturer – a task which may not be as easy as it sounds. Before you start, gather the relevant information. You need to know the make, model and year of registration of the car and ideally the vehicle identification number (VIN). Here Catch-22 may strike – if you haven't got a handbook, you may not know where to look for the vehicle identification plate: this is usually fixed in the engine compartment, but is generally somewhere prominent. The VIN is printed on the plate.

First stop is at a dealership that sells your make of car. Any dealer worth their franchise should be more than happy to locate a relevant handbook, although they sometimes make heavy weather of it. Or you can write direct to the customer services department of the manufacturer, the address of which you can get from a dealer or from the SMMT (see Address Book, p.121).

3. Learning to Drive *and learning about the car*

To be able to drive a car is one of the most liberating skills anyone can acquire. Even if the prospect of owning a car seems remote, being able to drive one is a very useful tool to have at one's disposal. But a car is potentially lethal, so learning to drive needs to be taken seriously. There are two stages in learning to drive. The first is learning to pass the test. The second goes on for ever. Good drivers never stop learning by experience.

'There is a maxim that to be seen on a bus after the age of forty is a sign of failure'

From the novel *More Home Life* by Alice Thomas Ellis

PASSING THE TEST

About half the people who take the test pass first time – women and men in roughly equal proportions. You must be at least 17 to drive a car on public roads (although if you are disabled and receiving a mobility allowance, you can start at 16).

The first essentials are a good instructor, and a suitable car. Although you can be taught to drive by friends and relations, it is rarely a good idea: it puts a lot of strain on the relationship, and on the car. It is definitely better in the early stages to use a professional instructor and the driving school's car. A professional won't (or shouldn't) panic when you make mistakes, groan when you grate the gears, or insult you in the way family and friends probably will.

Anyone who charges for giving driving lessons has to be approved by the Driving Standards Agency, which is responsible for maintaining basic standards, and must display an 'Approved Driving Instructor' identification sticker on the windscreen of the tuition vehicle. ADIs come in all shapes and sizes, and both sexes. Some teach in driving schools, and some operate independently. Sitting in a small car with a stranger can be an intimidating business, so it is important to ask around, and find an instructor or school known locally to be experienced and reliable. If you have no one to ask, choose a reputable driving school in your area which has a national reputation or is a member of one of the professional organisations.

There are increasing numbers of women driving instructors, but they are still a small proportion. However, no reasonable instructor will object to you taking a friend to sit in the back of the car during a lesson, if you are apprehensive about being alone in the car with an unknown man. Establish this before you book your lessons. When it comes to the driving test, you will only be allowed a chaperon if you need an interpreter because you are deaf, or do not speak sufficiently good English.

After a few sessions, most driving instructors will suggest that you have some driving practice in between lessons, although this is not compulsory and sometimes not even necessary or possible. When you practise, the person sitting beside you must have held a full UK driving licence for at least three years, and be at least 21. The car you practise in must be insured for a learner driver, and should have front and rear 'L' plates. Don't put them on the windows – they will get in the way.

There are residential driving schools which offer concentrated courses. These can work if you have some driving ability already, and could be worth trying if your time is severely limited. But it is better to absorb driving technique slowly so that it becomes habit.

If you learn to drive and pass your test driving a car with an automatic gearbox, your driving licence will only allow you to drive such cars. But if you pass in a car with a manual gearbox, you will be licensed to drive either type. Some older people learning to drive for the first time choose the automatic option because it shortens the learning process quite considerably, since you don't need to learn how to change gear. But the standard licence gives greater flexibility for most drivers.

AFTER YOU HAVE PASSED THE TEST

Now you can start to learn to drive properly. Because learner drivers are not allowed on motorways, your first experience of one can be a bit daunting. Most professional instructors with a motorway in the locality will give you an extra session on the motorway.

It is also quite possible to pass the driving test never having driven at night, or in the rain. Driving schools and instructors will give extra lessons to fill these gaps too. Or you can ask an experienced driver to come with you the first time you encounter these conditions.

The Institute of Advanced Motorists, RoSPA and DIAmond (see Address Book, p.121) offer advanced tuition and tests, and some car manufacturers run driving courses. There are several skid-pans around the country where you have your first skid in safety and be taught how to cope with it. Local road safety officers will know if there is one near you. Such a session makes an ideal present for a new young driver.

If you enjoy driving and can afford the time and money, it pays to improve your skill. Cars don't have accidents – drivers do.

THE HIGHWAY CODE

This slim volume is an essential part of driving knowledge both before and after you have passed your test. In the course of learning to drive you will have to memorise chunks of it, and you will be tested on it during the test. Don't throw it away or bury it in a bookshelf after the test because you will need to refer to it again.

LEARNING ABOUT THE CAR

The mechanics of the motor car are not unduly complicated and it helps enormously to have some basic knowledge while you are learning to drive. You should know some details about the car you own and drive, and some grasp of the essential components will help you to understand what people are talking about.

The heart of a car is the *engine*. Engines come in various shapes and sizes and may use any one of several fuels – petrol (leaded or unleaded), diesel, LPG (liquefied petroleum gas), electricity or in very rare cases, methanol. The size of the engines is expressed in litres (as in 3.0 litres) or cc's (cubic centimetres). Bigger engine capacities attract higher insurance premiums, because they are used in faster cars.

These days even quite small engines can be **turbo-charged** (see Glossary) for extra power and therefore increased insurance.

The engine develops power and passes it through the **clutch** to the transmission. The clutch allows the gradual application of power, and enables the driver to apply or disconnect the power at will. It also assists in gear changing. In a car with an **automatic gearbox** which has no clutch pedal, the clutch is an integral part of the automatic gearbox.

The **transmission** connects the engine to the road wheels via the clutch, gearbox (or torque converter and automatic transmission), and propeller shaft or constant velocity joints, depending on whether the car is front, rear or four-wheel-drive.

Constant velocity joints are steel balls housed in a cage and working in grooves, which allow the power to be transmitted to the front wheels of front-wheel-drive cars. **Back axles and rear hubs** pass the drive at right angles from the **propeller shaft** (usually described as the 'prop shaft') to the rear wheels of a rear-wheel-drive car.

The **differential** lets two wheels on the same axle revolve at different speeds.

The **engine** drives either the front wheels, the rear wheels or all four wheels. Most small cars these days are front-wheel-drive (FWD) partly because of the space-saving properties of the FWD layout, but also because they are easier for most people to drive, particularly in bad weather. You point the front wheels in the direction you want to go, and the rear wheels follow. On a rear-wheel-drive car – a format still favoured by manufacturers of some larger cars – the driven rear wheels push the car, while the front wheels steer it.

A four-wheel-drive (4WD) car has four driven wheels but is still steered by the front two.

4. Essentials
fuel, oil, water, tyres and wheels

To survive, cars, like mammals, need food and drink. The car's essentials are fuel – petrol, diesel or LPG (liquefied petroleum gas) – oil, water, and air for the tyres.

- ▶ Use the right fuel for your car.
- ▶ Keep the fuel tank topped up.
- ▶ Check the oil regularly.
- ▶ Unless the battery is 'sealed for life' check its fluid level at least once a month.
- ▶ Make a daily check on your tyres.

FUEL

Your car runs on either leaded or unleaded petrol, diesel (sometimes called DERV), or (rarely) on LPG or electricity. *These are not interchangeable.* Before you set off in a new car, or one that is unfamiliar to you, make sure you know what fuel it takes. The engine will be severely damaged if you do not use the right fuel for the car.

PETROL

Traditionally, lead was used as an additive to petrol to ensure smooth running of the engine. However, we now know that lead in the atmosphere is extremely harmful, so improved unleaded fuels (see Glossary) have been developed. All new cars on sale in Europe by autumn 1993 will be fitted with a catalytic converter (see Glossary) and must be run on unleaded fuel. Leaded fuel will ruin the 'cat', making the car fail its MoT test. Many older cars can be converted to run on unleaded fuel. Check with your garage.

Unleaded petrol comes in two 'strengths', called octane ratings – 95 and 98. The handbook will tell you which is best for your car. Unless specifically mentioned in the handbook, 95 octane can be used in all engines fitted with catalytic converters; 98 octane (which may be all you can get in some filling stations, particularly on the continent) will do no harm, but it costs more and there is rarely a performance advantage. Leaded fuel is usually 97 octane or four-star. Consult the handbook before you put leaded fuel into the tank.

DIESEL

This is increasingly used in passenger car engines because it is economical. It is particularly important not to let a diesel-powered car run out of fuel. Although some diesel engines behave like petrol engines in that if they run out of fuel you can tip some into the tank, others have fuel pumps that need priming before they work again. It is not a good idea to discover on the hard shoulder of a motorway which one you have. Read the handbook carefully.

The hoses and nozzles on fuel pumps are colour coded. Green indicates unleaded petrol, red is for leaded fuel, and black dispenses diesel. But beware: not all companies play the colour game. Octane (or star) ratings are also displayed on the pumps.

Remember – you must not put any leaded petrol into a car fitted with a catalytic converter: the car will still go, although not as it should, and you will ruin the 'cat'.

Putting unleaded fuel into a car which runs on leaded isn't a disaster, but the engine will protest with a lack of performance and the sound of 'pinking', which is a noise not unlike milk-bottle tops being shaken in a plastic bag.

If you put diesel into a petrol engine, or vice versa, the engine will not go for more than a few moments and you will get a bill for expensive repairs.

If the nozzle on the fuel pump does not fit into the tank, you may be trying to put the wrong sort of fuel into the car. Check.

Drivers of cars powered by liquefied petroleum gas get used to making sure that they keep the tank filled – LPG is not readily available, although it is getting more popular. But it doesn't come in cans, so you need to know where the next source is. Electrically powered vehicles currently run on batteries which need to be recharged from the mains at frequent intervals.

Precautions

Whatever powers your car, apart from electricity, fill the tank before the fuel gauge is down to one-quarter full. There is no excuse for running out of fuel. Running the tank to the last dregs can dredge up sludge from the bottom of the tank, which will clog up the works.

If you suspect that your fuel gauge is capricious, zero the trip meter (see Glossary) every time you fill the tank. Fill the tank when a quarter full, and note how many miles you have done. This gives you a rough guide to when the tank should be filled, even if the gauge is useless.

Almost all cars have the fuel filler at the back. Some are locked by a key, some are opened by a lever inside the car, some open at a turn and some drive you mad by twirling round interminably until you read the instructions. *Remember to replace the filler cap when you have filled up.* If you lose the cap, you can buy temporary ones at most filling stations. If you drive around without a filler cap you run the risk of getting water – from rain or a car wash – into the fuel tank, which will eventually stop the engine.

OIL

Running out of oil is more disastrous than running out of petrol. Running out of petrol will only stop the car; running out of oil will ruin the engine.

Most modern cars are fitted with an oil warning light (usually a picture of a dripping oil can), and if it comes on while you are driving you should stop the car as soon as it is safe. Older cars do not have this facility and rely on you checking the oil level regularly. Once a week is best.

Some cars appear to need very little oil. Others, often the older ones and the very high-performance models, need regular topping up. A weekly check avoids disaster. You will find a dipstick under the bonnet: this is a metal probe with a ring or hook on the end, and the handbook will show you where to find it. With the engine off and the car standing on a reasonably flat surface, arm yourself with a piece of kitchen paper or tissue and pull out the dipstick. Wipe the dipstick, push it firmly into its hole and then pull it out again. It has MAX and MIN marks and the oil level should be between the two. If the oil level is near MIN, add no more than half a litre or a pint of the appropriate oil.

Pour the oil into the filler under the bonnet, which usually has a large push-on or screw top, sometimes marked 'oil' or brightly coloured. You will find this on top of the engine. If you aren't sure, ask – putting oil into the wrong hole can have devastating results. When you have added the oil, don't expect to see the oil level through the filler. If you let the oil settle for a few minutes, and check again, you will know whether you need to add more. If you let the level go over MAX, the surplus oil will end up all over the engine.

The grade of oil your car needs is shown in the handbook. Oils are graded by their viscosity (thickness) at various temperatures, and labelled by SAE numbers. (SAE is a scale devised by the American Society of Automotive Engineers, and the reason it is used in the UK need not detain us.)

Most family cars use a multi-grade oil – SAE 10W–30 or 20W–50 – but some high-performance engines need a synthetic oil. Don't worry if you cannot get the brand name listed in the handbook – the important thing is to get the right grade.

As it is usually more convenient to check the oil when the car is standing at home, keep a small can handy for topping up. Don't bother to check the oil when the engine is hot, during a motorway run, for example. You will get a false reading. Wait until the engine is cool and the car has been standing for a while.

WATER

Water cools the engine. Some cars have sealed systems, which means that you do not need to top up the radiator. Others need regular checks. The handbook will tell you which your car has.

If your radiator needs water, *only remove the radiator cap when the engine is cold.* This also applies to the transparent reservoir (known as the 'expansion chamber' or 'header tank': see Glossary) which is marked to show whether you need to add water. Tap water will do. You can put water into the radiator until it is full, but the header tank has marks on it which tell you how much to add.

The cooling system also needs **antifreeze** which stays in the system all the year round. When the car was new, antifreeze was put into the system in the correct proportions. But if you have had to add water, which dilutes the antifreeze, remember to ask your garage to check the strength of the antifreeze before the first frosts set in.

Screen Wash System: water and some sort of additive is essential in the windscreen washer – the handbook will show you where the reservoir is. Keep it filled, and use an additive to clear the windscreen and prevent icing. You can buy screen-washer additive in sachets or more economically in bottles. As a short-term measure you can use a very small amount of washing-up liquid, but don't add antifreeze – it is highly corrosive and will ruin the paintwork. Oddly, you can be fined up to £1,000 if the washer bottle is empty, but if you let the radiator run dry so that the engine seizes there is no fine – just a very nasty bill.

Water in the Battery: although most new cars are fitted with a maintenance-free battery which is 'sealed for life', there are still plenty which require topping up regularly with distilled water (see Glossary). The handbook will tell you which your car has, and where to find it – some are to be found in unexpected places.

If your battery is the sort that needs attention, check it about once a month – more often in a hot summer. You will need a bottle of distilled water, available from garages or accessory shops. Once upon a time, it was suggested that water collected from the defrosting of a domestic refrigerator could be used to top up a battery. In fact such water is likely to contain foreign bodies, so this is not a good idea.

To top up the battery, turn off the ignition and locate the battery. Remove the panel on top of the battery or undo a couple of the screw tops. The fluid level should be visible just above the plates that can be seen inside the battery. Add just enough distilled water to cover them, and replace the cover or screw tops. If this isn't done regularly, the battery may fail you at an inconvenient moment, especially in winter when you will be using all the electrics.

TYRES AND WHEELS

Four patches of tyres, each no bigger than a page of this book, are the only contact a car has with the road – and unless that contact is perfect, the car can kill. These four patches have to transmit all the forces of the car – acceleration, braking and cornering – on dry, wet or greasy roads, as well as carrying the weight of the car and its occupants. Tyres must be given care and attention.

> Dorothy Levitt was nothing if not practical. In her book, *The Woman and the Car* (1906), she advised 'the lady automobilist' to carry a little mirror in the tool box. This would be useful, she wrote, to hold aloft from time to time, in order to see behind while driving in traffic.
>
> Rear-view mirrors did not come into general use until 1914.

▶ Are your tyres at the correct pressure?
▶ Have your tyres got sufficient rubber to make them legal and safe?
▶ Is the tyre on the spare wheel usable?
▶ Can you change a wheel if necessary?

Tyre pressures

You should check the tyre pressure at least once a month, even if the tyres look roadworthy. Appearances can be deceptive. A tyre that looks almost flat may be of the 'low-profile' variety, which are wider than they are deep, or it may be seriously underinflated. *You cannot tell by looking.* The only safe check is with a tyre pressure gauge: these are found in most garages. The handbook will tell you what the tyre pressures should be for your car. They are given in *bar* and *psi* (lbs per in²), and you will find one or the other clearly marked on the air line (see Glossary) at the filling station, depending on which country you are in and how modern the gauge is. A sticker with the pressures written on it, and put somewhere conspicuous, will avoid the necessity of ferreting out the handbook each time you check the tyres. If you have to fit new tyres, check the pressures with the fitter.

Pressures should be taken when the tyres are 'cold', i.e. before starting a long journey. The counsel of perfection is that you keep a tyre pressure gauge and foot pump at home. Unless you are a dedicated car owner you are unlikely to do this, and anyway most foot pumps are woefully inadequate. Check the pressures at a local garage, on the same air line each time so that you are not constantly faced with a different system, and do it when you are not in a hurry or wearing your best clothes. It is not difficult but can be grubby, and a pair of old gloves is useful, both for this and for wheel changing.

Unscrew the little dust cap from the valve on the tyre. Press the air hose firmly on to the valve and read the pressure on the gauge. Put each dust cap back when you have finished. Dust in the valve will make the needle valve stick.

Spare wheel

Do not forget the spare wheel. Although vehicle manufacturers have spent much time and effort devising ever more awkward places to hide the spare wheel, it needs to be kept in a usable state. The worst position is on a carrier under the car, where the wheel gets covered in muck. Some are under the floor of the boot, so that if you need to get it, the boot has to be unloaded. It is sensible to have a session at home when you get a new car, to find where the spare is and how to get it out. Even if you have no intention whatever of getting to grips with a spare wheel, you will at least be able to tell some good samaritan who stops in an emergency.

You may find that the inevitable nut which retains the spare has been over-tightened and needs brute force to free it. It is best to discover this before an emergency. Spray the nut liberally with WD40 (or some other penetrating spray easily found in hardware shops, garages and DIY stores) and tighten it yourself, so that you can be confident of being able to undo it should the need arise. However, it is of course important then to ensure the nut is tightened enough.

Tyre tread requirements

There are strict legal requirements for the amount of tread on tyres. Tread is the amount of rubber on the visibly patterned part of the tyre. All tyres – including the spare – *must* have 1.6mm of pattern depth over 76 per cent of the tread, with 'visible pattern' on the rest. It isn't much, and probably not enough. The RoSPA (Royal Society for the Prevention of Accidents) would like to see at least 3mm. New tyres have about 7mm, and the difference in the grip of a new tyre and that of one which borders on the legal minimum is dramatic, particularly in winter on wet and icy roads.

The penalties for running on worn tyres are fierce. If your car has worn tyres, you can be fined £2,500 and three penalty points *per tyre*. This means that you can lose your driving licence instantly if you are driving on four worn tyres – to say nothing of the spare. The Tyre Industry Council believes that one in seven cars in Britain is running on illegal tyres.

Because tyres are not cheap – you can pay upwards of £40 for one tyre – people hesitate before buying new ones. But saving on tyres is a very false economy. Because of the complexity of measurement, it is best to seek and take the advice of an expert at least once every twelve months. One pair of tyres, either front or rear, will usually wear more quickly than the others: for example on front-wheel-drive cars the front tyres, which do most of the work, will wear out more quickly than those on the rear wheels. And the spare, which may not have been used at all, will be quietly perishing in the boot. If a garage or tyre fitter recommends new tyres, don't assume that you are being asked to spend money unnecessarily.

Given reasonable care, a set of tyres on an average family saloon car could last up to 30,000 miles. Reasonable care means not only proper tyre pressures but also reasonable driving – avoiding potholes, kerbs and debris. Remember that what appears to be an innocent carrier bag in the middle of the road may contain half a dozen four-inch nails. Running over it could cost you a set of tyres, which won't be covered by insurance.

Punctures

Although punctures occur far less often than they used to (the industry reckons that a motorist can expect a puncture once very three years) they are by no means a thing of the past. Often a damaged tyre will deflate slowly so that you will be confronted by a flat tyre after the car has been parked for a while. If you run over something sharp in the road, a tyre may go flat immediately. If this happens, you will be aware of the car pulling strongly to one side or the other, and you may have to steer hard to bring the car gently to a standstill at the side of the road. Try to avoid braking hard.

Do not attempt to change a wheel on a motorway. The hard shoulder of a motorway is a hazardous place, not least because of the speed of passing traffic. Otherwise, if you have done some homework, conditions are favourable, and you are not alone, you may be able to replace the wheel with the spare. It is perfectly possible to change a wheel if you are alone, but it makes you an easy target for unwelcome attention.

Do you know where the jack is (see Glossary), and how to use it?
Is the car in a safe place, out of the way of other traffic?
Is the spare usable?

If the answer to any of these is 'no', you will have to get help. If the puncture has occurred on a motorway, it is best to drive very slowly up the hard shoulder and stop as close as possible to an emergency telephone. It won't do the punctured tyre any good, but it is much the safest thing to do and will save you a long walk.

Have a practice session at home. Make sure that you have a usable spare wheel and tyre. Then follow the instructions in the handbook, because the jacking system, which is used to raise the wheel off the ground, varies with every car. All handbooks cover wheel changing in some detail.

You may find that the wheel nuts are too tight for you to remove. When the car is built, the wheel nuts are tightened by air lines and they can be impossible to shift with the flimsy wheelbrace often supplied with the car. If you have a piece of steel tube which you can fit over the handle of the wheelbrace it will give you extra leverage and if necessary you can thump it with your foot to shift the wheel nuts. You can also buy telescopic wheelbraces, which amount to much the same thing.

As you remove the wheel nuts, put them in your pocket – *not* on the ground, where they can roll away or pick up dirt and grit which will make it difficult to replace them.

You can buy aerosol cans of pressurised foam which is pumped into the tyre via the valve to seal a hole. Don't. They are a very temporary measure if they work at all, and the tyre will be useless afterwards.

A few makes of car carry 'compact' spares, because they take up less space and are lighter. If your car has one of these it should only be used according to the manufacturer's instructions. These spares are only for emergency use and should be replaced as soon as possible.

Buying new tyres

If you need new tyres, the handbook will list the types of tyre recommended by the manufacturer. (When the car was designed, the engineers based it on certain makes of tyre.) But these are not the only tyres you can use. It is very important to buy tyres from an expert – an outlet which is a member of one of the trade organisations. Tyres need to be rated for the potential speed of a car and should have an 'E' mark, which indicates that they conform to EC regulations.

Early warning

Tyres are also an early-warning system. If they wear unevenly, it may be symptomatic of faulty wheel alignment, which can easily be caused by thumping a kerb, or something more sinister. Seek advice from a tyre specialist.

Running in a new car

For a new car or a car with a new or reconditioned engine there is only one hard and fast rule. *Never let the engine labour.* You will know by the sound it makes if this is happening. Driving too slowly in a high gear (third, fourth or fifth) will make the engine 'chug'. Change to a lower gear. Driving too fast in a low gear (first or second) will make the engine sound as though it is straining at the leash. Slow down or change to a higher gear. This is also a good rule to apply to your driving when the car is older.

Although the engine of your new car has been 'run in' at the factory, treat it gently for the first hundred miles or so. Then gradually increase its performance. This gives the moving parts a chance to 'bed in'.

5. Car Insurance

Motor insurance is complicated, but essential. If you drive a car, you must be insured because it is a criminal offence to drive your car, or let anyone else drive it, without insurance.

There are plenty of people who will offer you insurance – brokers, agents, motoring organisations, banks and (or course) insurance companies. Because women drivers are a better insurance risk than men, as they have less expensive accidents, some companies offer them a discount. Similarly, there are policies tailored for older drivers. On the other hand there are certain occupations, such as being a musician, a journalist or a jockey, whose claims are heavy and who are seen as bad risks. Consequently these people have to pay more for their insurance. Some companies give a discount to drivers who have passed an advanced driving test, and if you garage your car at night insurance will also cost you less, as it will if the car is insured for you only to drive. Drivers who do not smoke are eligible for cheaper insurance as research has shown that drivers who smoke in the car are twice as likely to crash as non-smokers. Even teetotal motorists who smoke have double the number of accidents of non-smokers, so some companies give a discount to motorists who sign an undertaking not to smoke in the car. Insurance for drivers under twenty-five can be expensive, particularly if they want to drive a high-powered car. Including them on a parent's insurance may be an economical alternative.

The sensible thing is to get several quotes and compare policies and prices before you make a choice. There is a wide variation in what you get for what you pay.

Don't wait until you have to make a claim before you read the policy. You are probably not as well insured as you think.

ROAD TRAFFIC ACT COVER

The Road Traffic Act requires all motorists to be insured against their liabilities for injuries to others (including passengers), and for damage to other people's property. The absolute minimum insurance is called Road Traffic Act cover. This means that only damage or injuries which affect someone else will be paid for by your insurance company. The cost of repairing you or your car will not be paid for by the insurance company. But you will be driving legally.

THIRD PARTY, FIRE AND THEFT

The next level – third party, fire and theft – adds fire and theft to the basic cover. So if your car is destroyed by fire (unlikely) or stolen (more likely), the insurance will cover it.

COMPREHENSIVE COVER

Two out of three private motorists take out so-called 'comprehensive' policies. Yet even such cover isn't totally 'comprehensive' – for example it will probably not cover the theft of things you leave in the car, even if the car is locked in a garage. However, this is the best you can get. Conditions vary from insurer to insurer, so it is vitally important that you read and understand the small print. A policy will specify the use to which a car can be put. Some policies don't cover the car being used for work – so minicabbing or delivery driving, for example, wouldn't be covered. (They need a special policy.) Most policies cover the policyholder while driving a car belonging to someone else, but *even under a comprehensive policy, if you are driving someone else's car, cover is limited to third party only, and accidental damage to the borrowed car will not be covered.* You will have to pay for damage repair yourself. If you have teenagers of driving age in the family who tend to treat property as communal, it is well worth sitting down and spelling out the insurance restrictions that apply to them and the car they are driving.

When calculating the cost of insurance, the company will want to know all sorts of things about the car and the people likely to drive it. It is advisable to be honest when answering. If you are economical with the truth, the insurance company can refuse to pay out when you make a claim.

There are now twenty different insurance ratings for cars according to which the insurers will also calculate the cost of cover. There used to be only nine groups, and it was easier to forecast, for example, that a turbo-charged sports car would be in the top group and cost more to insure than a Mini in the bottom one. Now that there are twenty groups it is more complicated. For example: Ford Escort groupings range from the Popular which is categorised as a Group 3, to the RS1600 belonging to Group 14 – with all the different engine variations in between. The new ratings are advisory, just as the old ones were, but in practice most reputable insurance companies use them.

It isn't only the performance of a car which is taken into account when a grouping is calculated. Some foreign cars are more expensive to repair than British ones, some take longer to mend, and some are more prone to theft. With car crime rocketing, some insurers will offer discounts for car alarms fitted by the manufacturer. Many policies include an 'excess' – a sum which you are liable for before the insurance company pays out. The higher the excess, the lower the premium.

NO CLAIMS DISCOUNT

The 'no claims discount' means what it says – if you have a claim-free insurance record, most insurance companies will reward you with a discount of 30 per cent after one year, which goes up annually. If you make a claim or someone makes a claim against you, the insurance company will reduce the discount, even if the accident was not your fault, because of the work involved in processing the claim. If your insurance company gets all the money back from the other insurance company they may let you keep your no claims discount, but don't count on it.

'KNOCK FOR KNOCK'

Very few accidents are entirely one person's fault, so some insurance companies have 'knock for knock' agreements with each other by which each insurer will pay for its policyholder's losses, regardless of who was to blame. The arrangement is intended to speed up the administration and get your car back on the road more quickly, but it can also jeopardise your valuable no claims discount. There isn't much you can do about this, although if you can prove conclusively that an accident wasn't your fault (i.e. you were at home in bed when someone drove into your car), you may be able to recover the costs in full from the other insurer and thereby salvage your no claims discount.

> The first lady racing driver was probably a Frenchwoman, Madame Laumaillé, who drove an 1898 De Dion in the 1898 Marseilles–Nice two-day event. On the first day she was fastest in her class and eventually finished fourth. Her husband came sixth.

DRINK/DRIVE

Apart from being a criminal offence, a drink/drive conviction is taken very seriously indeed by insurance companies. Convicted drivers will find that they face premium increases of at least 100 per cent when they return to the road, and indeed may find it difficult to get insurance at any price. The situation won't improve for several years – insurance companies have very long memories.

Insurance premiums rocketed during the 1980s, although in the UK they are still lower than in most European countries. Annual rises are commonplace, but you don't have to stick with the same company for ever. If you are faced with a massive price hike, it is worth shopping around again. You may find that the price you have been asked to pay is actually not unreasonable, or you may be able to save yourself money.

The onus is on you to tell your insurance company of any changes in the details you gave them on the proposal form – address, occupation, change of car, motoring convictions, etc. If you don't you may find that you have invalidated your policy, and the company won't pay out. *Compensation will certainly be reduced if you and your passengers are not wearing seat belts* both in the front seat and in the back if they are fitted there. A recent court case reduced a claim by £50,000 because the passenger who was injured in an accident had not been wearing a seat belt and was judged to have contributed to his own injuries. Telling that to passengers who refuse to wear a seat belt can have a salutary effect. The only exemption to the seat-belt law has to be supported by a doctor's certificate. These are rarely given.

CLAIMS

If you are involved in an accident in which someone is injured, you will have to produce your Certificate of Insurance (cover note) to the police. It is best not to keep car documents in the car in case they fall into the wrong hands, but it helps to keep a note of the insurance company's name and the policy number handy.

It will also be a condition of your policy to let your insurers know as soon as possible, even if you don't intend to make a claim. If your policy covers damage to your car, take the vehicle to a reputable repairer and tell the insurance company that you have done so. They may want to send an assessor to look at the damage before they authorise repairs. This is particularly important if the damage is such that the car may be written off.

If you have an accident involving someone who turns out to be uninsured, all is not lost. The Motor Insurers Bureau has a fund which compensates people who find themselves in this situation. You will certainly need a solicitor – preferably one who specialises in motoring law – and the process may take some time. If you cannot afford a solicitor, a Citizens Advice Bureau or local Law Centre will help.

6. On the Road

Motoring can be a stressful occupation. Some simple preparations will help to reduce the tension.

When you get a car, and before you take to the road, make sure you know your registration number, as you never know when you may need it. Next, equip the car with essential items. With the possible exception of a portable phone, these things belong to the car and it is wise to impress on those around you that they are not to be 'borrowed'. Otherwise, in an emergency you may find that something crucial is missing. Check the presence and condition of everything regularly. The following are basic lists. Add to them, depending on your needs.

In the car:
▶ the handbook
▶ a torch
▶ personal alarm
▶ paper and pencil/pen
▶ card with essential information
▶ money and phone card
▶ umbrella
▶ map(s)
▶ telephone or emergency call system
▶ roll of kitchen paper

- first-aid kit
- window scraper and de-icing spray
- a large sign that reads 'PLEASE CALL POLICE', which you can stick in the rear window or the open boot lid
- sunglasses, if you wear them regularly

In a sturdy cardboard box secured in the boot, keep:

- emergency triangle (see Glossary)
- old blanket
- can of fuel
- jump leads and tow rope
- waterproof coat, wellington boots or stout shoes and reflective band such as cyclists wear
- working gloves
- can of damp-repellent spray
- plastic bottle of water
- roll of waterproof tape

> 'Arachne travels to travel. Her only paradox is arriving somewhere, her only solution is to leave for somewhere else. . . . How can she explain her inordinate lust to drive, to cover road miles, to use up gas? There is no map for longing'
>
> From the novel *No Fixed Address: An Amorous Journey* by Aritha van Herk (Virago)

The handbook can live in the glove compartment with the torch but remember that batteries flatten whether the torch is used or not, and need to be renewed at intervals. If you leave them unattended too long the batteries may also leak and clog up the terminals. The best place for a personal alarm is in the pocket on the driver's door, so that it is always to hand. Sunglasses can be useful to block out blinding sun on the road.

Put important information – emergency telephone numbers (breakdown service, insurance company helpline, friend, relation or colleague who would be useful in an emergency), name of insurance company and policy number, make, model and registration number of the car, tyre pressures, grade of fuel and oil – on a card and stick it behind the sun visor together with some paper and a pencil, in case you need to note the details of an accident or leave a message.

The vagaries of our phone system and of parking meters mean that you never know what small change you will need. A bag of mixed coins and a phone card are essential. When you use them, remember to replace them.

Unless you are a trained first-aider, there is little point in carrying a paramedics kit in the car. But it *is* a good idea (and in some countries mandatory) to carry a small first-aid kit containing essential items. You can either buy one or make up your own. A plastic food box with a tight-fitting lid is an ideal container and you can fill it with plasters, antiseptic wipes, a crepe bandage, paracetamol, dry burn dressings, travel-sickness pills and scissors, together with any particular requirements you or your passengers are likely to have. *Warning*: the first-aid kit is the most frequently plundered item on the equipment list. Scissors in particular seem to grow legs and walk, so keep the kit in the glove compartment or, if you have no glove compartment, in a plastic bag wedged under the front passenger seat.

The best sort of window scraper is a plastic one with a sharp edge on one side and a foam rubber squeegee on the other. On fiercely frosty mornings the scraper, used in conjunction with a de-icer spray, will clear windows quickly.

DAILY DRIVING

Daily driving becomes a habit and it is far too easy, despite good intentions, to jump into a car every day without giving a thought to the car itself and what you are doing in it. Try to get into the habit of walking round the car every day to keep a check on tyres, leaks, body damage, etc.

► Is the car leaking? (Are there telltale puddles of petrol, water, oil or antifreeze underneath?
► Do the tyres look roadworthy?
► Is the filler cap in place?
► Are the number plates clear of mud?
► Are any of the lamp glasses broken?

The condition of the car is vital, but the condition you are in is important too. Everyone has 'off' days: for example pre-menstrual tension, headaches, flu, and the aftermath of childbirth, surgery, dental treatment or migraine can all affect your concentration and play havoc with your driving. So can some types of medication, a hangover or a serious emotional upset. If you genuinely feel under the weather it is much better to leave the car and find some other transport, or stay indoors. People may get irritated if you decide to break with routine and not drive, but remember that a motor car is a lethal instrument. Do not take chances. If you *have* to drive, be extra careful.

When you get into the car take a few seconds to check that you have all your belongings with you – that you haven't left anything on the road beside the car or standing on the roof – which can be easy to do if you are not feeling 100 per cent. As you start the engine, lock the doors, put your seat belt on and check the fuel gauge. If it shows less than a quarter full, fill up as soon as possible.

Driving down the same roads every day can lull you into false security and can have a mesmerising effect. You may have been taking the same route without incident for the past ten years, but that does not guarantee that every other driver is equally well disciplined. Consider varying your route.

Nine out of ten accidents occur within twenty miles of home, so even if you are just popping down to the shops, the risk is just as great as if you are setting off on a 200-mile trek up the motorway. Never allow yourself to become complacent just because you are on familiar territory.

Stopping distances

Drivers learn these by rote when they take the driving test, and promptly forget them. It takes longer to stop a car than you think it does. Shortest stopping distances and the recommended number of car lengths between you and the car in front are shown in diagram form on the back of the Highway Code. As a reminder, at 30 m.p.h. you need 75 feet or six car lengths to stop safely.

PARKING

Parking alongside the pavement has only recently joined the driving test requirements. Nevertheless, it still holds terrors for many motorists, some of whom will drive round for ages looking for a parking space that would accommodate a double-decker bus, never mind the average family saloon, rather than make a fool of themselves.

If you always drive the same car, practice will make parking easy. When you have found a parking space, which doesn't need to be more than three or four feet longer than your car, pull up parallel to the car parked in front and reverse into the space aiming for the middle of the gap. If you are parking in front of shops, you can use their windows as an additional mirror to show you how much room there is between your car and the cars in front and behind.

When parking space is limited, so is time, and you may get harassed by other drivers wanting the same space or who think you are taking too long to park in it. Fighting for a parking space seems to bring out the worst in all drivers, so try to ignore everybody else and concentrate on getting your car parked neatly. Sometimes it is tempting to go forwards into a parking space and then straighten up by mounting the kerb. This can damage the tyre, and even knock the steering out of alignment, and is not recommended. If you are parking 'end-on' to the kerb, or wall, always try to reverse into the space, so that you will be able to drive straight out.

Having found a space and parked in it, check that you are legally parked, and if you are on a meter put money in it before you depart. Sometimes the euphoria of finding a meter makes people forget this: your car can be clamped if you over-stay on a meter.

DRIVING AT NIGHT
The most important rule is to *use your lights so that you can see and be seen.* Some drivers seem reluctant to switch on dipped headlamps. Don't be shy of being the first driver to do so. Road and street lighting is patchy so always use dipped headlights when you are on the move, even in built-up areas, unless you are on an open road where you can use the full beam without blinding on-coming drivers.

If you cannot see as well at night as you think you should, get your eyesight checked. Even with perfect vision you cannot see as far at night as in daylight, so you should not drive as fast. The same applies to dawn, and particularly dusk when the light fades fast. Never drive so fast that you could not stop well within the distance you can see to be clear.

If you are blinded by the lights of an on-coming car, slow down and if necessary, stop. Try not to seek revenge by dazzling the offending driver and try not to dazzle the driver ahead. Your light beam should fall short of the vehicle ahead of you. If you are dazzled by the lights of a car behind, adjust your rear-view mirror so that the light is not shining in your eyes. Remember to correct it when the car has gone.

It is particularly important to lock the car doors from the inside, when driving at night. You could be stationary for a variety of reasons – traffic lights, hold-up on a motorway, or just peering at a road sign – long enough for someone to open a car door without you noticing.

7. Motorway Driving

Statistically, motorways are the safest roads in the country. In theory they are relatively straight and wide, well marked and signed, equipped with service areas and emergency systems, and regularly policed. They should be the motorist's dream. But many drivers find motorways intimidating, particularly the first few times they use them. Driving on a motorway is not a part of the driving test, and despite a network of about 6,500 miles many drivers encounter one very rarely, and some drivers never do. This means that the driver in front of you may well be making their first excursion on to a motorway, unnerved by the consistently high speeds and the high proportion of heavy goods vehicles. Keeping your car in good condition is particularly important for motorway driving, and lessens the chance of a breakdown.

Motorways have rules:

- ▶ The maximum legal speed is 70 m.p.h.
- ▶ You should drive on the left except when overtaking.
- ▶ You may not stop except in an emergency, even on the hard shoulder.
- ▶ Learner drivers, horses, pedestrians, cyclists and motorcycles under 50 c.c. may not use a motorway.
- ▶ No U-turns.
- ▶ No overtaking on the inside.

The first two rules are regularly broken. Although there are arguments in favour of higher motorway speeds, the legal limit remains at .70 m.p.h., and if drivers decide to exceed it, that is a matter between them and the motorway police. Indeed there are frequent occasions when 70 m.p.h. is too fast – in bad weather, particularly heavy traffic, or through roadworks.

There is no minimum speed on UK motorways, but crawling along a motorway at 25 m.p.h. for long distances is inconsiderate, unsafe, and frustrating for other drivers.

The second rule is often difficult to obey. The sheer volume of traffic in the left-hand lane can make it silly to keep diving into the gaps between the lorries, and then immediately out into the outside lane to overtake. You sometimes find a driver who insists on doing so, but such a driver is best avoided.

Drivers may overtake only on the right. However, it can happen, if the traffic is moving in queues, that the cars on your right are moving more slowly than you are. Even if this is the case, you *must not* move to a lane on your left to overtake, or *ever* use the hard shoulder for overtaking.

If you hog the middle lane of a three-lane motorway when the inside lane is free, you will drive other road users, particularly HGV drivers, mad with frustration. It is illegal to overtake you on the inside, and lorries may not use the outside lane. This sometimes results in angry drivers in vehicles only a few feet away from your rear bumper, which frightens you and does nothing to lower their blood pressure.

Look in your rear-view mirror frequently. Sometimes motorists aren't aware of the vehicle behind them because it is some minutes since they checked. Everything happens very fast at motorway speeds, so constant checks in the mirror are vital. You may think that the lorry driver who harasses you is mad, but it is safest to move over and let him be mad somewhere else. Similarly, if you are cruising at 70 m.p.h. in the outside lane and a car comes up behind you at 90 m.p.h. when there is room in the inside lane, move aside and let it go ahead. The fact that the driver is breaking the speed limit is none of your business, and you are more likely to cause an accident by sitting in front of them to prove a point.

BE ALERT

The key to motorway driving is *alertness*. The driver who reads the road ahead, as well as keeping an eye on the traffic behind, should not have problems. *The main cause of motorway accidents is lack of space between vehicles.* Every sort of driver, from HGV to small car, is guilty of this. The official advice is to leave one metre for every mile per hour between you and the vehicle in front, but this advice isn't very helpful, because judging 70 metres at 70 m.p.h. is difficult. A rule of thumb is to leave enough room for two cars to fit into the space between you and the vehicle in front. The trouble is, they probably will – and you will have to drop back. This is maddening, but less so than an accident.

When pulling out into a right-hand lane, look in the mirror. But bear in mind that mirrors do not show everything and that the car you are driving may have a 'blind spot' which conceals vehicles just behind and to the right or left of you. An additional quick glance over the shoulder will reassure you that the road is clear.

When you have overtaken, return to the left-hand lane as soon as possible, but don't cut in on the vehicle you have overtaken.

Keeping alert on a motorway, particularly on a long drive at night or in bad weather, is tiring. If you find your concentration flagging, stop at the next service area, or leave the motorway at the next exit. Stopping on the hard shoulder for a quick kip is not allowed, although the police may be sympathetic if you are taken ill.

'Luckily she had her Association Member's Card with her: luckily she had Sam's yellow-hooded cagoule to keep her dry. She hoped she was walking towards the nearest telephone: she had been told (but maybe it was folklore?) that motorway telephones were never more than half a mile apart'

From the novel *The Radiant Way* by Margaret Drabble (Penguin)

British motorways carry huge volumes of traffic. This destroys the surface, and so roadworks are frequent. If you see brake lights ahead, slow down. The vehicles may be slowing down because of an accident, or roadworks. If they appear to be stationary, put on your hazard warning lights before you stop and leave a couple of car lengths between you and the car in front. Strictly speaking, it is not legal to use hazard warning lights in this way, but it is better to

do so, and argue afterwards if necessary, than to have the car
behind pile into you. *See and be seen* is the rule.

BREAKING DOWN ON THE MOTORWAY

If the car starts to behave oddly, get into the inside lane, slow
down and look for an emergency telephone on the hard shoulder.
If possible, drive slowly to the next services area.

Emergency telephones are about a kilometre apart, and the inter-
vening markers have arrows showing the direction of the nearest
telephone. Stop as close as you can to the telephone, even if it
means driving on a flat tyre, or lurching uncomfortably using the
starter motor (see Glossary).

Try to get the car as far away from the carriageway as possible
and switch on the hazard warning lights, even in daylight.
*Whatever you do, don't reverse down the hard shoulder, and
don't run across the road to use a phone on the other side.* If you
have to walk, leave a note visible from the outside giving the time
and direction in which you are walking, and lock the doors before
you set off. *Don't try to hitch a lift, or get into a vehicle with a
stranger.*

Motorway emergency telephones do not need money or a phone
card, and you don't have to be a member of a motoring organisation to use one. The telephone connects you directly to an emergency operator who will be able to identify your position. When
you use the emergency telephone, stand behind it facing the
oncoming traffic, which will make you less conspicuous. Tell the
operator if you are a woman driver travelling alone, or with children or an elderly person. It is often hard to make yourself heard
on a motorway telephone because of the traffic noise, so don't be
afraid to shout or scream.

If you have to walk to a telephone, only you can decide whether
to take children with you, keeping as far from the road as possible,
stay with them on the verge behind the crash barrier, or leave
them with a responsible adult if there is one there. *Never leave
children in the car alone.* If you have pets in the car, leave a window open an inch or so for ventilation. After you have phoned, go
back to the car. If the weather is reasonable, sit on the bank or
verge. If an unidentified vehicle stops, get into the passenger seat
and lock the door. Most of the time the driver who stops will genuinely wish to help, but this cannot be guaranteed. A considerate

person will recognise that you are nervous and will not be offend-ed if you talk to them through a slit in the window.

You are more likely to be killed or injured by sitting in a station-ary car on the hard shoulder than you are to be attacked. If no res-cue vehicle appears within 30 minutes, call again, and again, and again. A breakdown vehicle should have your name and a police car should be easily recognisable as such; the occupants will pro-duce identity cards. Treat with suspicion any unmarked car or van that stops. It isn't always polite, but no reasonable person will be offended.

LIGHTS

Never hesitate to use your sidelights or dipped headlights if you are driving in anything other than perfect conditions. However, it isn't considerate to follow another vehicle with your headlights on full beam, or to leave high-density rear fog lights on in clear weather.

8. Long Journeys

With fuel tanks in many of today's cars offering upwards of 350 miles between fill-ups you can, in theory, drive all day without a stop. But it isn't a good idea, even for very experienced drivers. The car may run like clockwork, but the driver doesn't, and you will become increasingly lethargic without noticing it.

Fatigue is surprisingly difficult to recognise – it creeps up on a driver and undermines the concentration long before he or she actually feels sleepy. There are some precautions to take which will make a long drive safe and pleasant.

- ▶ Are you and the car in good condition?
- ▶ Have you checked tyres, fuel, oil and water?
- ▶ Is everyone sitting comfortably?
- ▶ Have you planned a route and have you got maps?
- ▶ Is the luggage sensibly packed, with things you may need easily available?
- ▶ Is your motoring organisation membership up to date?
- ▶ Have you checked the emergency kit?

Try not to be tired when you set off. This is easier said than done if you have had to plan and pack for a long trip, but try to avoid eating a huge meal before setting out and, of course, no alcohol. It is better to sleep, and leave at 5 a.m. than to leave at midnight after a hard day. In the early morning the natural light will improve, whereas if you leave in the afternoon, the dark will come down on you and make driving more tiring. Too many accidents are caused by drivers who fall asleep at the wheel.

'In my first few years at Pittman County Hospital I was able to help Mama out with the rent and the bills and still managed to save up a couple of hundred dollars. With most of it I bought a car, a '55 Volkswagen bug with no windows to speak of, and no back seat and no starter. But it was easy to push start without help once you got the hang of it, the wrong foot on the clutch and the other leg out the door, especially if you parked on a hill, which in that part of Kentucky you could hardly do anything but. In this car I intended to drive out of Pittman County one day and never look back, except maybe for Mama.'

From the novel *The Bean Trees* by Barbara Kingsolver (Virago)

No matter how experienced a driver you are, try to plan the journey so that you have a break at least every three hours or 150 miles. A five-minute break when you get out of the car, take a few deep breaths and stretch your legs, will help to restore your circulation and concentration. Even stopping for petrol will break the spell, but the deep breaths will not be of the highest quality.

PASSENGERS
A passenger can be a help on a long journey, but not necessarily so. If you have nervous or critical passengers, a long drive can be particularly stressful. Encourage them to sit in the back and talk to each other, rather than to you. But an observant passenger who can sit in the front and help with the navigation, and who, noticing when the driver is beginning to flag, can demand a comfort stop, is worth their weight in gold.

Hitchhikers
Never give a lift to hitchhikers, no matter how deserving they seem. It is unfortunate, but the risk is too great.

Even if you know the route like the back of your hand, always carry an up-to-date road map in the car. Traffic jams and diversions are all too frequent, but you can very often navigate round them with the help of a map.

If the route is unfamiliar, it can be reassuring to spend some time planning it in advance, and writing road numbers and landmarks on a piece of paper which you can stick on the dashboard for reference.

Forward planning means not having to stop and ask the way. If you are lost, especially at night, stop and ask for directions somewhere which is well lit and where there are likely to be plenty of people – police stations, filling stations, hotels and hospitals are best. If you ask a pedestrian or passing motorist for help, check that your car doors are locked and only open the window sufficiently wide to allow conversation. *Never* allow a stranger into the car on the pretext of showing you the way, no matter how harmless they may seem.

PACKING THE CAR

One of the joys of travelling by car is that you do not need to pack everything neatly into suitcases light enough to carry for miles across airport concourses or station platforms. But if you fling everything into the boot, remember that in an emergency you may have to empty it all to retrieve the spare wheel.

Luggage on a roof rack requires thought. Fitting the roof rack itself, unless your car has an integral one, can be a fiddly business and shouldn't be left until the last minute. Secure luggage on to it with great care. Not only is it dangerous for things to fly off the roof into the road, but if you lose a suitcase it will almost certainly be the last you see of it and its contents.

FOOD

Eating *en route* can pose problems. It is best to get out of the car and walk about, but restaurants at motorway service areas can be busy and noisy which is not necessarily what you want. For the family, a picnic is ideal, but if the weather is bad you may be forced to eat it in the car, which isn't what you want either. If you can afford the time, look for a quiet café or pub (no one objects these days if you don't drink alcohol) away from the main road or motorway. Planning helps – there are several guides which will point you to somewhere suitable.

If you pack a picnic, remember that savoury food is better than sweet stuff, which makes people thirsty. Similarly, unsweetened drinks are preferable. If you carry sweets in the car for refreshment while driving, remember that they are no substitute for proper food on a regular basis and some people find that eating sugary things when they are already tired actually increases the fatigue. And fatigue is dangerous.

If you are travelling with a baby, pack enough bottles, nappies etc. to see you through if you get stuck in a lengthy traffic jam. If you are breast-feeding, take fluids for yourself.

EXERCISE

Sitting in the same position for a long time, either as driver or passenger, can be a muscle-binding business. Some simple exercises can relieve tension and revive circulation. If you are driving, do them during a break or when the car is stuck in traffic – *not* on the move. They should not hurt, but if one does, stop.

▶ *hands and feet*: rotate your hands and feet (not necessarily at the same time), several times in each direction. Punctuate by scrunching and then stretching your fingers and toes.

▶ *neck*: drop your chin on to your chest and let your head feel very heavy. Roll your head slowly in a half-circle from shoulder to shoulder, several times. Clasp your hands on the back of your head and *very gently* pull your head down.

▶ *bottom*: clench your buttocks hard several times in quick succession. This will make you look as though you are bouncing up and down in your seat. At the same time pull your stomach in and hold for a count of five.

▶ *shoulders*: put the palms of your hands on the front of your shoulders on the same side. *Gently* push your head back, at the same time pushing your elbows back. Slowly reverse the process.

▶ *more shoulders*: put your right hand over your right shoulder and twist your left hand up between your shoulders blades and try to touch your fingertips. Then do it the other way round.

▶ *legs*: clasp your hands around one knee and pull it gently up to your chest, several times. Repeat with the other leg.

face: make the worst faces you can devise using every facial muscle including your tongue, and stretching them until you think your skin will split. This is particularly popular with children.

LAVATORIES

These are few and far between on main roads and motorways so always take the opportunity to use one when you stop, and if you have passengers encourage them to do the same. Stopping on the side of the road for a quick pee is not wise, and on a motorway, illegal.

9. Motoring Alone

In general it is much safer for a woman to drive alone, day or night, than to walk down a poorly lit city street. A lot of publicity has been given to the dangers faced by women alone in cars, but millions of women drivers all over the country drive around every day and come to no harm. With sensible precautions there should be no serious reason for women to worry about driving alone.

Lady Jeune, whose husband the Rt. Hon. Sir Francis Jeune, KCB was one of the pioneers of motoring in Britain, had advice for women motorists in 1903.

'If women are going to motor, and motor seriously – that is to say, as a means of locomotion – they must relinquish the hope of keeping their soft peach-like bloom. The best remedy is cold water and a rough towel, and that not used sparingly, in the morning before the start'

One wonders what advice she would give to today's motorists.

The first and most obvious precaution is to have a well-maintained car with petrol in the tank so that it doesn't break down.

Simple checks should be carried out by all car owners. Never be put off by people who say that a car is complicated. It isn't. There are several commonsense things you can do to make your motoring life worry free.

▶ Get a handbook for the car and read it; then keep it in the glove compartment.
▶ Join a motoring organisation.
▶ Keep the doors locked when you are in the car.
▶ If you can afford it, get a mobile telephone, AA Callsafe or RAC's ET: if not, you can buy an imitation telephone handset which will fool people into thinking you have a carphone on which you are calling for help.
▶ Leave a spare ignition key with someone who is readily accessible.
▶ If you can, and unless you run the risk of worrying them unduly let someone know where you are going and when you expect to arrive, or return. Then if you go missing, people will know where to start looking.
▶ Buy two personal alarms of the screeching variety – keep one in the pocket of the car door, the other in your handbag or coat pocket.
▶ Never give lifts except to people you know well.
▶ Park in well-lit and well-populated areas.

JOIN A MOTORING ORGANISATION EMERGENCY SERVICE

If you are in trouble your first priority is to get in touch with someone who can help. Joining a motoring rescue service is the best way. Sometimes membership comes free with a new car, but if so remember to renew it when it runs out.

Membership of the major organisations offers a variety of options; depending on how much you pay, you can have a service which starts the car outside your front door, carries out basic repairs, or rescues you when you are far from home. You get what you pay for. If you have young drivers in the family, you will get peace of mind by extending your membership to them. But remember, *joining a motoring organisation is no substitute for keeping your car properly serviced and maintained*. Indeed some organisations penalise members who call them out too frequently to a car which is obviously unroadworthy. Nevertheless, economising by not having a rescue service membership is a false economy.

LOCK THE DOORS

When you get into the car, *check that all the doors are locked*. Locking the doors from the inside should become as much of a routine as putting on a seat belt. Indeed in some US states, it is a mandatory part of the driving test. Don't be perturbed by people who say that if the doors are locked no one will be able to get you out if you have an accident. Accidents that necessitate someone needing to open the door from the outside *are very rare indeed*. If necessary, rescuers will smash a window whereas if you leave the doors unlocked someone can open the doors when you are stationary or slowing down and climb into the car, or grab you, your child, handbag or briefcase. Some people recommend locking car doors only in urban traffic. But cars are stopped for a variety of reasons, even on motorways, and you are unlikely to develop the habit unless you *lock the doors every time you get into the car*. Central locking has made this much easier, but if your car does not have central locking, check that all the other doors and boot are locked before you get into the car and lock the driver's door. Clearly there is less risk if you have a car full of people, but good habits won't do any harm. Locked doors will open from the inside, although if you have childproof locks (see Glossary) on the rear doors they can only be opened from the outside. It is not unknown for thieves to open the boot lid at traffic lights and be away with anything interesting before you realise what is happening. If your boot lid or tailgate has a push-button catch, make sure it is always locked with a key except when you are actually opening it.

MOBILE PHONES

Having a telephone is obviously a good idea for a woman alone. A phone which you can remove from the car is most useful and less tempting to thieves. If you have equipped the car with the recommended list, you should have all you need.

STICKERS AND THINGS

One hazard faced by women drivers comes from people who want to draw them into conversation about their car. It helps if there is no talking point. Avoid eye-to-eye contact, and do not open the window to talk to anyone you don't know. Just shout if you want to. It may seem harsh, but it is sensible to denude the car of all stickers apart from those which come with security devices, or essential parking permits. Any sticker which announces that you have seen the lions at Longleat or some such or, worse still, something potentially provocative suggests that you are someone who is happy to chat about these activities, and you are asking for trouble. Even 'Baby on board' or 'Dog in the car' gives an opportunity for someone to press their unwelcome attentions on you. It is a good idea to get rid of anything inside or outside the car that might attract attention, or that advertises the fact that the owner is a woman. It is always best to keep the inside of the car clear of rubbish, whatever your gender.

DANGERS

It sometimes happens that a passing driver will point to your car, indicating that there is something wrong with it. This might mean that you have forgotten your lights, or that a door is open. Do not stop to check until you are in a safe place.

Sometimes a driver will indicate by sign language that you pull into a lay-by or car park. Don't do this. They may genuinely be trying to help, but if there is something seriously wrong with the car – a flat tyre or an oil leak – you will already have noticed it. *Do not stop until you have reached some well-lit area where there are plenty of people around*. Deserted lay-bys, dark pub car parks or the more remote parts of motorway service areas even in daylight are not safe. No reasonable person will criticise you for ruining a tyre or – which is most unlikely – an engine in these circumstances.

PARKING

When you park, especially at night or if you will be returning to the car in the dark, try to find somewhere prominent. By the kerb, try to park close to a street light. In a car park, reverse into a parking space whenever possible because it will be easier to drive away. In a multi-storey car park, get as close as you can to the pay booth, or to a ramp where there are more likely to be other drivers. If a car park is full it is tempting to go to the top or bottom floors where there is often more space for manoeuvre, but these floors may be deserted when you return. In open-space car parks at stations and airports, try to park as near to the exit or a bus stop as possible.

When you leave the car, make sure that there is plenty of space between you and the other cars for the doors to open, and check that the steering lock is engaged. (If you wiggle the steering wheel you will hear a click, after which the wheel will not move. This means that the steering is locked and can only be unlocked with the ignition key.) Don't forget to close all the windows and lock the car – one car in five is left unlocked – and if it is likely to be dark when you return, take the torch with you.

When you go back to the car it is best to have the car keys in your hand, so that you can unlock the car and get in without having to rummage for them. A car key can be an effective weapon. If you are nervous, tell the attendant at the pay booth that you are going to collect your car, and where it is.

It is often tempting to park illegally. This can lead not only to a hefty fine, but also to being clamped. You can even be clamped if you overstay on a meter. The unclamping procedure means that you have first to contact the clampers and pay the fine, which can be approximately £100 and then wait with the car until the unclamping team arrives. At busy times, or at night, this could mean that you will be alone in the car for hours, which is not pleasant. Consider the possibility before you leave the car.

MAD DRIVERS

It is rare but possible that someone will try to run you off the road. Lone female drivers are particularly at risk from those who think it fun to frighten them. Usually such idiots will get bored if you keep a steady moderate speed in the inside lane, and ignore them. Just occasionally they persist. Try to pay no attention, and avoid eye contact.

If you have a mobile phone, pretend to use it now. The possibility of being caught usually deters such people. If not, stop at any convenient point. On the motorway stop at the next service area and drive into the petrol station, where there will certainly be people. On an ordinary road, if necessary drive to the nearest well-lit house and park in their drive. Don't be afraid to scream. The sort of people who get their kicks from frightening women drivers are usually cowards and do not want to end up in court. Be warned – they are not always men.

If another driver does deliberately force you to stop, try not to panic. Don't turn off the engine, but make sure that the doors are locked and the windows closed. If the driver gets out of the car and comes towards you, reverse your car and drive away. If this is impossible, turn on the hazard warning lights, sound the horn and if you have a personal alarm or car phone, use it. By law you should not carry anything which can be construed as an offensive weapon, but if someone does manage to get a door open or a hand through the window, it is most unlikely that you would be prosecuted for fending them off with a squirt from a de-icing spray or a scratch with a window scraper.

ALONE ON THE MOTORWAY

If you have to use an emergency motorway phone, stand behind it and face the oncoming traffic. This makes it easier for you to be heard by the operator, and you can also see if anyone is approaching. Statistically you are more likely to be injured by sitting in the car on the hard shoulder than you are to be assaulted. But if anyone pulls up, even if they appear to be police or breakdown services, get into the car and lock the doors. A bona fide policeman or mechanic will understand and will show you some identification.

The emergency telephone on a motorway puts you directly in touch with Motorway Control. Tell them immediately that you are a woman on your own and your call should be given priority. After you have given the operator the necessary details, repeat that you are a woman on your own. You do not need money for the phone and inside the door of the telephone box you will find a list of all the information you will be asked for. *Don't worry if you don't know all the details.* All they actually need to know is your location, which is printed on the phone, the colour of your car, and your name. The name is important so that when help arrives you can check that the mechanic knows who you are.

TAXIS

Most taxis are safe and reliable, but it is better to call one from a phone than to hail one in the street, unless you are fortunate to be in a city such as London where you should be safe with a 'black cab'. Minicabs are not allowed to tout for business on the street. The law prevents women-only minicab firms advertising for women drivers only, but many firms do employ women and you should insist on one if you are nervous.

10. Dressed for Driving

FOOTWEAR

Footwear is crucial. Although it is just possible to control a car in high-heeled shoes or wellington boots, there are very good reasons for not doing so. Consciously or unconsciously, a driver gets a good deal of information about the car and the driving conditions through the feet, and so thick unbending soles or unbalanced shoes with stiletto heels are hard to drive well in. Racing drivers wear light leather shoes and some people find it best to drive barefoot, particularly in summer. Driving barefoot is an excellent way to keep cool on a very hot day and much less dangerous than wearing floppy sandals.

Another good reason for not driving in your best shoes is that even low-heeled shoes get badly scuffed. Some people keep a pair of driving shoes in the car and change every time they drive, but this is indeed a counsel of perfection, and not really practical if you are wearing lace-up boots and hopping in and out of the car every five minutes. If you do have a spare pair of shoes floating around the car, keep them out of the footwell on the driver's side. A rogue shoe can too easily creep under the pedals and cause a nasty accident.

Another hazard is shoes that slip on the pedals, perhaps if they are wet or have smooth plastic soles. Part of the problem may be worn pedal rubbers, and if so it is easy to replace them. If the shoes are at fault, banish them from the car. There are few things

The two world wars had lasting effects on women in the motoring world. With most able-bodied men fighting in Europe, it fell to women to build, repair and drive vehicles of all sorts. In 1916 the length of women's skirts rose permanently above the ankles, probably because driving ambulances and dustcarts would have been difficult in skirts that trailed on the ground. One social historian regarded this change in fashion as 'an indication of woman's liberation from her subordinate role'. If so, such liberation was short-lived. The inter-war years saw most women motorists back in the passenger seat.

CLOTHING

If you are uncomfortable in the driving seat you will probably drive badly. Whoever invented the 'car coat' clearly never drove a car, because being trussed up like a chicken in a thick woollen jacket which scarcely reaches the thighs is about as uncomfortable as you can get. So too is the ubiquitous anorak. Layers of light clothes, which can be added or subtracted, are much more effective. You may start a trip feeling cool and wearing several layers, only to heat up as the drive continues. Stop at the next convenient point to remove a layer or two, and in the mean time turn the heater off and open a window. Trying to take a sweater off while driving and wearing a seat belt is dangerous.

SIGHT

Nothing is more important to a driver than sight. If you normally wear glasses to drive, keep a spare pair in the glove compartment so that if you lose or break your usual pair, you will not be stranded. This is compulsory in some European countries. Similarly, if you wear contact lenses, carry an emergency pair of spectacles in the car. It is also useful to have a pair of sunglasses in the car. Sun can cause glare and headaches not only in summer but also in winter when the sun is low in the sky, especially if the road is wet with recent rain.

11. Breakdowns and Rescue Services

There are two sorts of breakdown. In the first, the car stops and in the other it won't start.

If your car stops or refuses to start somewhere where it's safe, you are lucky. Before you do anything else, try to get the car out of the way of other traffic – into a lay-by or on to a verge – and switch on the hazard warning lights. Then, if you are carrying an emergency triangle, put it in a prominent position about 50 metres behind the car.

There are countless causes of a breakdown. Some are simple and unforgivable like running out of petrol or losing the keys, and some so technical that they can't even be fixed by the breakdown service. Before you panic, ask yourself some basic questions:

▶ Have you run out of fuel?
▶ Has the safety switch been triggered?
▶ Where are you? Roadside phones and callboxes have a location printed on them: the operator will ask you for it.
▶ Are you a member of a breakdown service?

Motorway breakdowns, which we deal with separately, are relatively straightforward. On motorways there are telephones with locations on them. Elsewhere there may not be.

WHAT IS THE PROBLEM?

Even if you only have a little mechanical knowledge, you may be able to get the car going, or at least diagnose the problem so that you can decide what to do.

Have you run out of petrol?

Running out of petrol is inexcusable, but sadly all too frequent. It also makes you feel extremely stupid. If you anticipate difficulty in finding suitable fuel or are one of those people who likes to live dangerously and run around on the last tablespoonful of fuel, carry a can of fuel in the boot. Suitable cans, which don't leak, are on sale at accessory shops and some garages. Buy one that carries a British Standards Institute label.

If you run out of fuel and have to persuade a garage to lend you a can, you may well find that it is an old oil can with no spout. It will be very difficult to get the fuel into the filler without wasting half of it or pouring it over your shoes, unless you can find a piece of stiff paper or card to roll into a makeshift funnel. Sometimes garages demand a deposit if they lend you a can – if you have no cash they may ask for a piece of jewellery or a credit card. Better to carry a spare can in the boot.

Has the safety switch been activated?

Some cars are fitted with a fuel system safety switch which is designed to shut off the fuel supply in the event of an accident. These switches can be triggered by mistake if you go over a bump too quickly or hit a kerb. 'Sleeping policemen' (see Glossary) will sometimes activate them. The handbook will tell you if you have such a cut-off switch, and where it is. Resetting the inertia switch is a matter of moments and requires no mechanical knowledge.

Is the battery flat?

If an engine will not start, the most likely problem is that the battery has no power. This is more likely to happen if the car has been standing for several days in wet and cold weather. A battery in good condition should not be affected, but leaving the lights or radio on will flatten even a new battery in a few hours. Even if you are carrying jump leads (see Glossary) you now need help. Starting a dead engine with jump leads needs another power source, usually that of another car but sometimes just a battery.

First of all, check with the handbook that your car is suitable for starting with jump leads, and that the battery providing the power is the same voltage as the one in your car.

It is quite possible to jump-start a car by yourself, but it is a lot easier with two people. Locate the batteries in both cars and manoeuvre the host car so that you can reach both batteries. The cars should be as close as possible without actually touching – you don't want to weld them together. If possible switch everything off in both vehicles to lessen the drain on the batteries, although at night you will need some warning lights.

Connect the red lead first to the positive (+) terminal on the charged battery, and then to the positive terminal on the flat battery. Then connect the black lead to the negative (–) on the charged battery and finally to a metal bit of the engine with the flat battery, or the negative terminal (check with the handbook). Start the car with the charged battery and rev it hard for a few moments. Then start the other car and run both vehicles for a couple of minutes before disconnecting the leads. Reverse the order in which you connect them, black first and then red, being very careful not to let the leads touch each other or any metal bits of either car.

Don't switch off the engine with the newly charged battery until it has been running for at least half an hour – more, if you are using lights, wipers, etc.

Sometimes it is possible to bump-start (see Glossary) a car by towing or pushing it – but *not* if your car has an automatic gearbox or a diesel engine; nor, in fact, any car with a catalytic converter if its engine is warm. If you can find someone who will help to tow or push your car, sit in the driving seat, turn the ignition on, release the handbrake, depress the clutch and put the gear lever into third gear. When the car is going as fast as your assistants can achieve, let the clutch out, and with any luck the engine will fire. At this point, if the car is being towed, remember to steer round the tow car. Do not let the engine stall. It is not a good idea to let a total stranger drive your car in an attempt to start it. You may never see either of them again.

Is there steam coming from under the bonnet?
If so, stop the car somewhere safe, turn the engine off and resist the temptation to lift the bonnet and investigate until the steam has subsided. There are various causes of overheating and most of

them need professional repairs. If you are carrying the necessary bits and pieces, such as sticky tape and a gallon of water, you might be able to make a temporary repair on a split hose. But the days of fashioning a fan belt out of a nylon stocking are long gone. Occasionally, flying plastic bags or leaves block the radiator, causing the engine to overheat, and the problem should be solved when you clear them.

Before you put water into the radiator, the cap should be cool enough for you to put your hand on it comfortably. *If you take the radiator cap off while the engine is hot you will probably scald yourself.* Release the cap very slowly, allowing any steam or accumulated pressure to seep out gently.

Is there smoke or flame coming from under the bonnet?

If so, you do not stop to diagnose the problem. Get everyone out of the car and as far away as possible, as quickly as possible. Don't bother about the luggage, just grab the baby or grandma and your handbag – and *run*. Call the fire brigade to deal with it.

Have you got a puncture?

If the car starts to steer in a strange way, of if there is an unusual thumping, you may have a flat tyre. Drive gently to a safe place or, if you are on a motorway, close to an emergency telephone. Get out and look. If you are on an ordinary road not too close to passing traffic, and feel competent to do it, change the wheel. (For tips on how to do this, turn to 'Tyres and wheels', p. 26.) Otherwise, call a breakdown service.

Has the windscreen shattered?

It takes a lot to shatter a windscreen, but very occasionally they craze in front of your eyes. It is a disconcerting experience. Forget anything you may have read about punching a hole in the glass. By peering through the glass you should be able to steer the car on to the verge or hard shoulder. Stop, turn off the engine and put the hazard warning lights on. You now have to decide whether to drive on with a hole in the windscreen or call a specialist windscreen service. Unless you are in a frantic hurry, get someone to come and replace the screen. It isn't cheap, but with luck it will be covered by your insurance. Specialist firms will replace a screen without leaving bits of glass all over the place.

If you must get somewhere immediately, stuff some newspaper or tissues into the demister slots on the top of the dashboard, and then find some gloves or a sleeve to protect your hand. Push the glass gently from the inside out, so that the fragments will not fall into the car. Push out as much glass as you can before driving on slowly. It is best to wear glasses to protect your eyes from bits of glass blown out of the screen. Don't drive any further than you absolutely must with the windscreen in this condition.

Has the engine got wet?

Some engines are susceptible to damp. If the starter motor turns when you turn the ignition key, but the engine refuses to start, a liberal spray of water repellent (see Glossary) may help. Open the bonnet and spray the contents liberally around the central part of the engine. Unless it is raining or very damp, do not close the bonnet. In either case wait about five minutes before you try to restart the engine. It may not work, but it's worth a try.

Has a fuse blown?

The car's electrical system is fused in much the same way as a domestic circuit. If the lights, windscreen wipers, horn, indicators or other electrical components have suddenly stopped working, it is possible that a fuse has blown. This is where you need the handbook and the torch. The fusebox will be either under the bonnet or around the dashboard. The handbook will identify it and indicate the appropriate fuse. You will be able to tell by looking at it whether it is faulty – the wire inside it will be broken, as it is in a domestic electric light bulb. Most fuseboxes carry spare fuses but if not, 'borrow' one of the same rating from another function. For example, if the windscreen wipers (essential) have packed up, you can probably use the fuse from the radio (nice but not crucial) circuit. Remember to replace it as soon as possible. If the replacement fuse blows too, something more fundamental is wrong and a garage will need to sort it out.

Have you lost your car keys?

Lost keys don't exactly constitute a breakdown, but many breakdown call-outs are to people who have locked their keys in the car, or lost them down a drain. (It is a proven motoring fact that if you drop car keys into a gutter there will be a drain at your feet.)

If there are keys inside the car, someone will be able to get them out – if the worst comes to the very worst, by smashing a window. Knowledgeable people with a criminal turn of mind can break into some cars with a bit of wire coat-hanger or a screwdriver, but the criminals have drawn attention to these facts and security is now becoming so sophisticated on some of the newest cars that only the most professional car thief can gain entry. If you have a car with a built-in burglar alarm which is activated when you lock the door, the whole neighbourhood will be witness to your careless-ness and probably not very pleased about it.

If the keys are well and truly lost, you will need to know the key number to get a replacement. Keep a note of the number in your diary. New cars come with two sets of keys; it is wise to leave the spare set with someone who is usually contactable, and get a third set to keep at home. A remarkable number of car owners leave the spare keys in the glove compartment, which doesn't make a lot of sense.

WHAT DO YOU DO NEXT?

If you cannot identify the problem, or cannot rectify it, you need to call a breakdown service, which will want to know where you are. Stranded motorists often do not know where they are, which makes finding them very difficult. If you can identify landmarks and road numbers, it will help considerably.

If you haven't got a carphone, the AA's Callsafe, the RAC's ET (Emergency Telephone) or a Citizens' Band radio, you are now faced with a problem for which there is no perfect solution unless you have broken down within sight of a telephone. You can walk in search of a phone, you can stay by the car and flag down a pass-ing motorist, or you can put your 'PLEASE CALL POLICE' sign in the rear window and wait for something to happen. If you decide to walk, leave a note visible on the dashboard saying in which direction you have gone, and at what time.

Things are more complicated if you have small children or an elderly person with you. You may not want to leave them in the car while you go for help, especially if the car is stuck at night in a vulnerable spot, and they may not be able to walk for miles looking for a telephone or a garage. Only you can decide the best course of action.

It is *extremely unwise* for any motorist, particularly a woman, not to be a member of a breakdown service. Like other forms of insurance, you may never need it. But if you do break down, such a service is invaluable.

> The Second World War once again saw women in demand as drivers. Princess Elizabeth (now HM Queen Elizabeth II) went through a highly publicised course of car mechanics, as if to prove that internal combustion was not a mystery understood only by men. This time women abandoned the skirt, of whatever length, in favour of trousers – the heiress to the throne having been photographed in dungarees, thus making them socially acceptable.

Although motoring organisations offer a wide variety of products, not all of them motoring-related, their *raison d'être* is to rescue you when your car breaks down. When the chips are down, you want an organisation that will find you quickly and repair the car, or take it and you home or at least to a place of safety. Some organisations offer all sorts of ancillary services – insurance, legal advice, maps, guides and touring information, driving schools and goodness knows what else – which you may or may not want. They vary considerably in cost and in the service they provide – although in some of the more remote parts of the country the same garage will be called out for members of all of them. Which do you choose?

Do you want cover for yourself in any car, or for a specific car?
Do you want help if your car breaks down outside your front door?
Do you want to include a second car, a caravan or a motorbike?

The market leaders are the AA, RAC, National Breakdown, Britannia, Autohome and Europ Assistance. The Guild of Experienced Motorists (see Address Book) also operates a scheme whereby you call out a garage and pay the bill, and GEM reimburses you. Prices vary widely and depend on the sort of service you want. Competition between the various organisations is lively, and they vie with each other over the speed of response, which is good news for the consumer. There are also special schemes operated by organisations like the Caravan Club and the Environmental Transport Association (see Address Book).

Assuming that you haven't been given a free membership when you bought your car, the best plan is to collect the relevant brochures and decide what sort of service is best for you and your bank balance.

Several of the schemes encourage members to pay by direct debit. Although direct debit is not universally popular, at least if you use it to pay for a breakdown service you will not find yourself stranded because your subscription has run out when the time comes to use it.

Phone

All emergency services have one thing in common: you have to get in touch with them by phone, and you have to know where you are.

If you have broken down with no phone in sight, you will have to find one. It may need money or it may need a phone card. Be armed with both.

An alternative is a mobile phone or carphone. With one of these you will be able to contact the police, an emergency service, or even a friend or relative. Although prices are coming down rapidly, such phones are still not cheap, but they provide a lifeline for motorists. There are areas of the UK where reception is poor or non-existent so you will not be able to use them everywhere.

The same is true of AA's Callsafe and the RAC's ET (Emergency Telephone). Callsafe is a direct line to the AA so that if you break down you can contact a control room immediately. You buy a Callsafe unit (about £200 plus a monthly subscription of about £10). Calls are free. Callsafe is packed in a carrying case which you take with you in any car you happen to be driving. When you need it, plug it into the cigarette lighter and punch in a number, either for the AA control room where an operator can talk to you or for the emergency services. Women drivers are given priority. You can lend the unit to sons and daughters or use Callsafe to report accidents, and you can use it in any car. But you will need to tell the operator where you are, and if you have a total electrical failure or a blown fuse, Callsafe will not work.

The RAC's ET is a normal transportable carphone which incorporates two dedicated buttons – one calls the emergency (999) services and the other connects you directly to the RAC control room, but again you will have to tell them where you are. ET costs approximately £200 to buy, the line rental is around £15.00 a month. Make sure you know what the charges are per minute for cheap rate and business hours.

It will be five years or so before a nationwide satellite-based emergency system which automatically pinpoints your location will be available. Even if you don't know where you are, the system will locate you instantly and call the emergency service you need. The technology exists already, but until there are communication systems that cover the entire country we shall have to wait for its introduction.

12. Accidents

The bang, the crunch or the dull thud – each is a nightmare. You have hit something, or something has hit you. What do you do?

- ▶ STOP.
- ▶ Switch off the ignition, put on the handbrake and hazard warning lights and take a couple of slow deep breaths to steady yourself.
- ▶ Assess the situation before you get out of the car – try not to panic. As the driver, you are in charge.
- ▶ Is anyone hurt? That includes you and your passengers, as well as any other road user.
- ▶ *Don't move injured people* unless they are in immediate danger from fire. *Never remove the helmet of an injured cyclist or motorcyclist.*
- ▶ Ask someone to call 999 (on a motorway use an emergency telephone).
- ▶ Evacuate uninjured passengers to a safe place well away from the traffic.
- ▶ Ask other drivers to turn off their engines and put out any cigarettes.
- ▶ This sounds heartless, but may be crucial. Resist the temptation to say 'sorry' – even to your passengers. When in doubt, don't say anything. If there is an insurance claim, anything you say may be interpreted as an admission of guilt.

Stopping after an accident is essential. By laws which have grown up over the years, you must stop if you are involved in an accident in which someone is hurt or in which an animal (horse, cattle, ass, mule, sheep, pig, goat or dog) is involved. You must also stop if you damage roadside property. You don't have to stop if you run over a cat or a deer, though if you hit a deer you will probably have stopped anyway! If you do not stop, you could later be charged with an offence.

> 'All Londoners know there's a close connection between driving a car and the impulse to murder.'
> Jane McLoughlin, *Evening Standard*, 1988

People involved in accidents react in various ways, but a lot shout abuse as a way of releasing tension. Don't get involved in an argument. If you can stay calm and authoritative, you will be far more use. Make sure that the emergency services are not needed – if they are, a carphone is invaluable. If you are in an accident in which the police become involved, you must stay at the scene until they say you can leave.

Don't attempt to move someone who is injured, and don't let anyone else move them either, unless there is the unlikely risk of fire. It is easily possible, unless you are medically trained, to make an injured person far worse if you move them without knowing what you are doing. More important is to make sure that other traffic is aware of the incident by putting out an emergency triangle. If someone needs to warn approaching traffic, they should wear the fluorescent band (which you should always carry in case of emergencies) or something light-coloured.

If you have an accident you must give your name and address to anyone who is involved, including the police. If you don't do this, you must report the accident to a police station within 24 hours, and must bring along your insurance certificate. You should also make a note (which is why you should always carry paper and pencil in your car) of the name and address of any driver involved, as well as the registration number, colour and make of their cars, or the names and addresses of anyone who saw the accident and is prepared to help. You should also ask the other driver for details of his/her insurance company.

Even if no one has been injured you should *call the police if you suspect that the other driver has been drinking*. Be prepared to be breathalysed yourself. Otherwise if the accident is a 'minor' one – i.e. where the damage is limited to cars which are not causing an obstruction and the road is not blocked – the police are unlikely to be interested. If you can make a rough sketch of the road and the position of the vehicles it will help when it comes to an insurance claim. Most insurance companies give their clients a form to keep in the car, which you fill in if you have an accident. *Which?* magazine produces a useful card to keep in the car on which you can record details of your insurance company, next-of-kin, and so on.

As soon as practicable you should get in touch with your insurance company even if you do not intend to make a claim, because the other party might. It is sometimes tempting to try to do a cash deal with the other driver but even if you do, they may still decide to proceed with an insurance claim, leaving you having admitted responsibility by handing over money.

If your car is drivable, you will get to your destination. But if your car if too badly damaged to drive it will have to be removed. In a severe accident, the police will arrange this. In a minor accident you may have to do it yourself, and the motoring organisations will be helpful.

FIRST AID

Unless you have had first-aid training, there is only a little you can do for people injured in an accident:

▶ Do not move an injured person unless there is serious risk of fire.
▶ Call the police and an ambulance.
▶ Make sure that the injured person can breathe freely, by loosening clothing.
▶ Staunch serious bleeding by pressing on a wound with a clean handkerchief, towel, pad of tissues or anything similar.
▶ If someone is unconscious, check that they are breathing and gently tilt the jaw back to clear the airway.
▶ People often suffer shock in an accident and it takes various forms – sweating, shivering, rapid breathing or sickness. Try to keep them warm and quiet until help arrives.
▶ Do not give an injured person anything to eat or drink.

13. Winter motoring

PREPARING THE CAR FOR WINTER

During October and certainly in early November, prepare your car for winter. No matter if you live in the middle of town and only use the car for the school run, winter can catch you out. Several manufacturers offer a winter check, and it is worth taking advantage of this. If not, this is a good time to have the car serviced. Battery, tyres and windscreen wipers need special attention, as does the antifreeze. A battery which is already declining can be dealt a terminal blow by a cold snap, leaving you stranded. Windscreen wipers need replacing every twelve months, or more frequently if they have been used a lot. If tyres are reaching the legal limit of tread, now is time to consider replacing at least two of them. And of course the washer bottle needs to be kept full of water and an additive which will prevent it freezing up.

Antifreeze

Antifreeze is added to the water in the car's cooling system to prevent the engine and radiator freezing solid, which would result in major inconvenience and expense. The strength of the antifreeze in the cooling system needs to be checked, especially if you have had to put any water in during the year.

Lights

Check all the lights regularly. This is easiest with an assistant who will walk round the car as you operate the lights, to ensure that all are working. Remember the brake lights, indicators, fog lights (if you have them) and reversing lights. (You can do this by yourself if there is a convenient wall or garage door, but it's a fiddly business.) Even if you clean nothing else on your car, give the lamp glasses a regular wash. On dark winter nights you need all the illumination you can get, and even a thin film of muck can drastically reduce the strength of a light. Equally important is the fact that other people need to be able to see you.

Winter equipment

Put a de-icing spray in the car if you have not got one already. When the car is covered with frost or snow, you will need to clear all the windows and door mirrors before you set off, in order to avoid the 'porthole' hazard (peering through an inadequately small clear patch). Heated front and rear screens are designed to do this for you in a couple of minutes, so if you have them be patient. But if your car is not fitted with them, a bucketful of very hot water with a handful of kitchen salt dissolved in it, thrown on to the windows, will do the trick. It doesn't matter how hot the water is. People will tell you that this will crack the screen. Don't worry – it won't.

If you live in an area which can expect wintry conditions, it also helps to add a spade and a couple of old doormats to your emergency kit. If you are stuck in snow or on an icy road, the old doormats pushed under the driven wheels (in the unlikely case of a four-wheel-drive car getting stuck, the wheels that are spinning), should give you enough traction to get going.

If you are travelling with small children or elderly people – who feel the cold very quickly – put an extra blanket, or better still a duvet, in the car so that if you get stuck in the snow they can be kept warm. Don't forget it can be useful to keep a small pair of sunglasses in the car as in winter the sun is low in the sky and can easily dazzle the driver.

DRIVING IN BAD WEATHER

It's never fun, but sometimes it has to be done. If the weather is really foul – fierce winds, black ice, snow, dark and fog in any combination constitute 'foul' – ask yourself whether this journey is

You can see snow, but not what it conceals, and you cannot always see ice. Sometimes the road just looks wet; the impression that the car is running abnormally quietly is often a danger sign.

If you must drive in bad weather, leave yourself plenty of time for the journey. On any road, but particularly motorways, *leave a lot of space between your car and the vehicle in front*, and *drive slowly and steadily*. On slippery roads, keep all your movements – steering, braking, accelerating and gear-changing – as smooth and gentle as possible.

Fog

Fog can be very distorting, as well as patchy. Some people imagine that they can see well in it, and drive too fast. The effect of head-lights on fog can be to turn the fog into a wall in front of you, so use front and rear fog lights if you have them, but only dipped headlights. Use demister and windscreen wipers. Sudden patches of fog, sometimes freezing, can blind you so it is better not to be driving too fast. If you switch on rear fog lights, remember to switch them off again when the weather clears. *In dense fog, if you can see the car in front of you, you are too close*.

> 'Men are more nervous passengers than women, and they tend to prod the floor intermittently, searching desperately for the brake pedal. This floor banging becomes irksome on a long journey, but there is nothing to be done unless you go in for violence and hit the offender with a spanner'
>
> From *What Every Woman Ought to Know* by Joyce Wilkins (Newnes 1969)

Skidding

Among the techniques which are not required to pass the driving test is how to handle a skid. This means that your first experience of a skid will be for real, and that your immediate reaction will be to stamp on the brakes and swing the steering wheel. Neither will help. A skid happens because the tyres have lost their grip and because the driver was braking, accelerating or cornering faster than the conditions would allow.

If you find yourself in a skid, the conventional advice is to 'steer into it'. This is not much help if you don't know which way your wheels are pointing but means that if you can, you should try to steer the car *in the direction in which it is actually going* for a couple of seconds, and then gently steer back in the direction you want it to go. If you are driving a front-wheel-drive car you may be able to control the skid by pointing the front wheels in the direction you want to go, and accelerating gently.

If you live in an area prone to snow, ice, rain, or mud on the roads, which is hilly and has long winters, you should consider three possibilities that will make your winter driving less hazardous: buy a car which has four driven wheels (known in the trade as 4 × 4, or four-wheel-drive); choose anti-lock brakes; and buy winter tyres. Although it doesn't matter how many driven wheels your car has, if all four are slithering on ice, a four-wheel-drive car doubles the chances of being able to get a grip on some part of the surface. Anti-lock brakes sense in milli-seconds when the wheels have locked under braking. The system automatically releases and reapplies the brakes far quicker than a driver can – several times a second – to provide grip and safe braking as well as allowing the driver to steer. Winter tyres have deeper tread and special tread patterns to cope with snow and mud. None of these is cheap but if you regularly drive in bad weather it is worth considering any or all of them. Studded tyres are fitted by drivers in alpine countries. These are expensive and of limited use in Britain because on clear roads they skid or tear up the surface, and we cannot be guaranteed three months of snow and ice as in parts of Scandinavia. Snow chains fitted to your normal tyres, which you can buy or hire, could keep you moving. They are not the easiest things in the world to fit, so have a practice at home in the dry.

Floods

Water on the road needs to be treated with great caution even if it is only a deep puddle, but with care you should be able to negotiate all but the deepest floods.

▶ Keep a good distance from the vehicle in front of you so that your car is not drenched by its spray or bow wave.

► Drive slowly – modern tyres are designed to disperse water, but do not ask too much of them.
► Drive through the water where it is shallowest; if you must drive through deep water, move very slowly and steadily in first gear. The faster you drive, the more water will be forced into the engine compartment and the engine will be flooded.

It is sometimes recommended that you let someone know when you leave and expect to arrive, but this has to be a matter of personal choice. Telling an elderly person when you expect to arrive may cause them great concern if you don't turn up when you say you will.

14. Signs and Signals

SIGNS

Britain's road are littered with signs of all sorts. There are signs giving orders, signs giving warnings, direction signs, information signs, road markings and vehicle markings.

As a general rule, signs giving orders are mostly circular and those with red circles indicate something you must not do. Signs with blue circles but no red border mostly give positive instructions. Triangular signs are usually warning signs, but not all warning signs are triangular. Motorway signs are blue, but many other signs are blue as well.

To guide you through this automotive jungle, get a copy of the latest *Highway Code*, which shows many of the signs commonly in use, or better still a booklet called *Know Your Traffic Signs* also published by the Department of Transport and on sale in bookshops.

Knowing the significance of white markings on roads is important, because breaking the rules that apply to them constitutes a driving offence. Recognising the yellow parking restriction lines could also save you from being clamped.

SIGNALS

The driving test no longer asks for hand signals, but knowing them comes in handy if you are being towed, or have a faulty light. Make any hand signals clear and positive. An arm protruding from a driver's window on a hot summer's day is usually only an indication that the window is open. Signals are covered in the *Highway Code*.

The linguist Deborah Tannen writes in *You Just Don't Understand: Conversations Between Women and Men* (Virago), that asking for directions is one of the many conversational tasks that women and men view differently, and that consequently cause trouble in talk between them. She demonstrates with an example:

'Sitting in the front seat of the car beside Harold, Sybil is fuming. They have been driving around for half an hour looking for a street he is sure is close by. Sybil is angry not because Harold does not know the way, but because he insists on trying to find it himself rather than stopping and asking someone. Her anger stems from viewing his behaviour through the lens of her own. If she were driving, she would have asked directions as soon as she realised she didn't know which way to go, and they'd now be comfortably ensconced in their friends' living room instead of driving in circles, as the hour gets later and later. Since asking directions does not make Sybil uncomfortable, refusing to ask makes no sense to her. But in Harold's world, driving around until he finds his way is the reasonable thing to do, since asking for help makes him uncomfortable. He's avoiding that discomfort and trying to maintain his sense of himself as a self-sufficient person.'

15. Towing and Being Towed

TOWING

If you have never towed anything behind a car, it is best to start with a lesson. The Caravan Club gives courses to non-members as well as members, and even provides a caravan, though not insurance. The trouble is that you could easily find yourself in a situation where something has to be towed here, now and by you, without an instructor in sight.

Towing something attached to a rigid tow-bar isn't difficult, but like other forms of driving it needs common sense and anticipation. Your car will feel heavier than usual, and the combination of car and trailer (or another car) will be longer, higher and wider than you are used to. The wheels of the trailer follow the car, so unless you swing wide on corners to compensate, the trailer will cut across the road and hit anything that happens to be there. Braking and manoeuvring distances are greater, and you will need to watch out for bridges and gaps, overhanging trees and gateways. Make sure that the mirrors are properly adjusted before you set off.

In both cases don't be afraid to drive slowly and steadily. To avoid a string of frustrated drivers building up behind you, pull into a lay-by or car park every so often and let them all go past. Until you get the knack of it, reversing can be tricky and it helps to have someone guiding you. The trick is to start by turning the steering wheel *in the opposite direction* to that in which you want the trailer to go. Once the trailer is going in the right direction, put the steering wheel on to the opposite lock, so that the car follows the trailer.

> Isadora Duncan did not have much luck with cars. Her two children (Deirdre and Patrick, aged 8 and 2) were killed when the car in which they were travelling with their governess rolled into the Seine, drowning them all.
>
> In 1927 Duncan was eager to buy a Bugatti 37. The car was brought to her in Juan-les-Pins for a demonstration by a good-looking Italian mechanic who worked locally.
>
> Before she left on the test-drive Duncan said to a friend: 'Can't you see that he's not a chauffeur – he's a Greek god in disguise. And that is his chariot! Goodbye – I leave for glory.'
>
> She got into the car, wrapping her red-fringed scarf round her shoulders. After only a hundred yards, the car stopped. The crowd saw that the fringe of the scarf was caught in the spokes of the wheel. Isadora Duncan was dead, strangled by her scarf.

Towing a broken-down vehicle on a tow-rope is best left to a professional but if you have to do it, work out a system of signals with the person in the towed car. Tie something eye-catching in the middle of the tow-rope so that pedestrians won't trip over the rope.

BEING TOWED

This will only happen if your car has broken down. (Note that it is illegal to carry passengers in a caravan or trailer which is being towed.) If you have to be towed, make sure it is by someone who knows what they are doing, and with a proper tow-rope attached either to the towing eye on each car or to a substantial part of the chassis – *not* the bumper or the steering arm. The handbook will help. The ignition key will need to be turned so that the steering, brake lights and indicators will work.

If you are being towed by a breakdown vehicle, the mechanic will give you instructions. Try to keep the tow-rope taut but not tight, and don't brake unless you have to. Don't try to start a car by towing if it has a catalytic converter, automatic transmission or diesel engine, or a combination of these, as for different reasons in each case, it will ruin the car.

The speed limits for cars towing caravans or trailers are 30m.p.h. (built-up areas), 50m.p.h. (single carriage-ways) and 60m.p.h. everywhere else.

16. Car Care

A car is a potentially lethal machine, and needs to be kept road-worthy, both for your safety and the safety of others. Cars need more care and attention than most domestic appliances, but good care is repaid severalfold. A washing machine needs little maintenance but if it doesn't get it, it won't break down on a motorway in the night. Your car might.

Routine checks and servicing are very simple if you follow the instructions in the handbook to the letter. They may seem excessive, but if your car lets you down, remember that it may be your fault.

BASIC MAINTENANCE
Daily checks

Walk around your car every day and check:

▶ *tyres*: Do they look roadworthy?
▶ *leaks*: Are there unusual puddles under the car? If so, 'Essentials' will help you to identify them.
▶ *lights*: Are all the glasses intact?

Inside the car:

▶ Is the fuel level below one-quarter? If so, fill up.

▶ Is the windscreen washer reservoir at least half full? If not, replenish with water and additive.

Every time you fill up with petrol

▶ Check the water and oil levels. The handbook shows you where and how.

Monthly checks

▶ Check the tyre pressure, including the spare.
▶ Are all the light bulbs functioning?
▶ Check the battery fluid and brake fluid levels. See handbook.

Recognising warning signs

Never ignore warning lights on the dashboard, unusual noises, a sudden drop in fluid levels or uneven tyre wear. If in doubt, consult your garage immediately.

There is no standardisation of controls and instruments and virtually every model differs in some way, but as a general rule red warning lights demand immediate action, yellow ones are less urgent and a blue light indicates that your headlamps are on main beam.

The handbook describes the symbols on your dashboard, and what you should do if they illuminate. Read the handbook carefully so that you can identify each light, and what it means. *It is never wise to assume that it is the light itself which is faulty*. The pictograms to watch out for particularly are the dripping oil can, the brake disc and the battery. If any of these come on, stop as soon as it is safe to do so. The 'oil can' warns that the oil pressure is low. Check the oil with the dipstick after the car has been standing on a level surface for a few minutes, and if necessary top up the engine oil. If there appears to be sufficient oil, but the warning light is still illuminated when you restart the engine, do not drive the car. An engine starved of oil, for whatever reason, will seize up and be ruined.

If the brake warning lights illuminate, stop the car as soon as you can and check the brake fluid level. There is a brake fluid reservoir under the bonnet. The handbook will show you where, and how you check the level.

If a brake warning light illuminates while you are driving, which happens very rarely, it may mean that one of the brake circuits has failed, leaving you with inadequate braking. While you are looking for somewhere safe to stop, leave more space than usual between you and the other vehicles, because the car will take longer to slow down and stop. If the braking is seriously affected, do not drive the car, but call for help.

If the 'little battery' lights up (except when you are starting the engine) it probably means that the battery is not charging. Switch off all unnecessary electrical equipment, and drive to the nearest garage for help.

Keep an eye on the temperature gauge, particularly when you are driving in slow, heavy traffic. The gauge is your early warning of overheating. If you have let the water level in the radiator fall dangerously low, or if a hose has split and dumped all the water on the road, the engine will overheat. If you drive with the car in this state you will seriously damage the engine.

Leaks

Often after a frosty or very wet night, water drains off the car and stands in pools around it. This is perfectly harmless – it is pools under the car which you need to keep an eye open for.

If you find an unusual, serious pool of anything under the car, it may mean that something important is leaking. Green or yellow fluids suggest a radiator leak. Red is probably hydraulic fluid from the braking system. Clear fluid is either water or petrol – stick your finger in and sniff. Oil is sticky, dark and difficult to get rid of. Check the relevant fluid levels. You can top up with oil or water, which will get you to a garage. But if the braking system is leaking, call a garage for help before you drive the car.

SERVICING

Regular servicing is essential for the maintenance of a car. A thorough service should be carried out annually, or every 12,000 miles, and should include a tyre check and a brake safety check. The windscreen wipers should be renewed once a year, or every 12,000 miles, although this is not always included in the standard service. If you buy a new car from a garage near you, you should take it back there when it needs attention.

The handbook will tell you exactly when your car needs servicing. To keep within the warranty, you need to adhere to the manufacturer's service intervals. But don't wait until the day before the

warranty expires to take the car back for a major service and recti-
fication of any niggles which may have presented themselves. Give
the garage about a month's leeway before the warranty runs out.

When you take a car to a garage you cannot expect the staff to
have extrasensory perception. Book the car in at an off-peak time
so that you will have time to talk to the service receptionist and/or
the mechanic who will be looking after your car, and explain what
you would like them to do. Even if you don't know what is wrong,
you can explain the symptoms – a strange noise, or an unusual feel.
It is no good booking a car in for a service and expecting the
garage to guess what is bothering you. It helps if, before you go to
the garage, you write down the points you want to raise, give a
copy to the mechanic or service receptionist, and keep a copy
yourself. That way you won't forget something in the heat of the
moment, and the garage won't forget either. If necessary, and a
road test is not included in the service schedule, suggest taking the
car for a short run with the mechanic so that you can demonstrate
the problem.

You should ask how much the work is likely to cost. Many
garages have fixed prices for various jobs, but make sure they can
get in touch with you to authorise the expenditure over an agreed
amount *before* they start the work.

If you want to collect the car after business hours, the garage
may offer to leave it on the street with the keys hidden somewhere. This is not a good idea. You should collect the car from the
staff in the garage, in plenty of time to check the state of the car,
examine the bill, and if necessary give the car a short test-run with
the mechanic. You should certainly not wander round the neighbourhood looking for your car in the dark. Apart from the safety
factor, it is too easy for misunderstandings to arise about any damage the car might have.

Some women car owners feel nervous about garages. Certainly
the atmosphere can be intimidating, and there can be a lot of wait-
ing around in unfriendly surroundings and the feeling that you
haven't been taken seriously or, worse still, that you have been
ripped off. Fortuantely more and more dealerships are coming to
realise that women represent nearly half their business, and that
they need to be treated with respect, and while you won't find
many garages with women mechanics, there are increasing numbers of female service receptionists. When you deal with a garage,

try not to be either wimpish or aggressive. If you do not understand what is being said, don't be afraid to ask for an explanation.
If parts have been replaced on the car, ask for the worn parts to be
returned to you. If you feel you are being given the run-around,
simply take the car away. There are plenty of garages. When you
find a good garage, one you feel confident with, stick to it. The better the relationship between you and the garage, the safer your car
will be.

If you come across a garage that treats you badly, try to make
time to write a letter of complaint to the chairperson, or to the
manufacturer involved. Things only get better when we make a
fuss.

John Bolster, one of the most eminent British motoring
writers of the century, had a formidable mother. In 1904 she
bought a 6-cylinder Napier, a marque associated with one of
the great motoring names, S.F. Edge, known to the British
public as 'Mr Motoring'.

John Bolster recalls his mother's car: 'It was a dreadful car. It
had mechanical troubles galore and was a martyr to
overheating, while it seldom ran for long on all 6 cylinders.
Then the paint and varnish started to peel off the *Roi des Belges*
body and my mother decided to show it to the great Mr Edge.
She waited for some time and then the celebrated personage
came down the steps from his office; in total silence and
ignoring the owner completely, he stalked once round the car
and then returned whence he had come.

A few minutes later, a secretary brought a note saying: 'Mrs
Bolster may have her Napier repainted by any good
coachbuilder of her choice, at my expense. S.F. Edge.'

The moral of this story is that it is always worth
complaining.

DIY car maintenance

Many local authorities give evening classes in car maintenance
especially for women. These are a very good way to learn about
the subject. At a garage near you, you may also find one of several

car maintenance sessions for women, or women's workshops sponsored by car manufacturers or oil companies. Being free, these are good value and are designed to build confidence, increase understanding and improve personal safety. They often provide a woman driver with the first opportunity to change a wheel or check tyre pressures under supervision.

If making a living as a car mechanic appeals to you, many colleges and polytechnics run courses that lead to apprenticeships. These will also engender a greater confidence in you and your car.

WASHING AND CLEANING
Exterior
Having spent a lot of money on a car, it makes sense to keep it clean and tidy – and it needn't take a lot of time. Fortunately for us, the automatic car wash has made it possible to keep the visible parts of the car free of corrosive dirt. Purists shudder, and maintain that a bucket of water, shampoo, wax and elbow grease are the only proper necessities for a clean car and that car washes damage the paintwork. Not so. The paint finish on today's cars will not be improved by waxing, nor will the car-wash brushes damage it. Only the paintwork of a very old car needs washing by hand.

If you use a 'drive-in' car wash (the sort with revolving brushes) check that the radio aerial is retracted. If you forget, the aerial may be torn off and get tangled in the brushes, causing nasty scratches on the car, and you will have the expense of replacing the aerial. Some aerials unscrew, some go down when the radio is switched off, some you have to push – consult the handbook. You shouldn't use this sort of car wash if there is a temporary roof rack fixed to the car, but the permanent ones found on some estate cars pose no problem.

Some garages have 'jet' washes – where you direct a powered jet of water at the car. They take longer than automatic car washes but are usually cheaper because you do the work yourself. They are wonderful for very dirty cars, particularly shifting mud from the wheel arches and removing the salt residue from under the car after winter, but you need strong arms and a pair of wellington boots. Using a jet wash may be the only chance you stand of persuading children to wash the car. It is very easy to soak the brakes so after using a jet wash *be careful to test the brakes two or three times before driving back on to the road.*

Most automatic car washes offer a choice of washes. There is no need to spend money on waxing and hot-air drying. Keep a chamois leather in the car and dry the windows when you come out of the wash. The rest of the car will dry itself. (If you keep a real chamois leather in a plastic bag it will go slimy and end up smelling like a sewer. Buy one of the very good imitations and let it dry naturally after use.)

If you wash the car at home, the secret is to use plenty of water, a proper car shampoo (washing-up liquid makes a lot of foam but doesn't shift the grease, despite what they say in the ads), and a large synthetic sponge. A floorcloth in one bucket of water will merely redistribute the dirt and grit. Pay special attention to the headlamps and rear lights. The glass can get very dull and reduce the light they give.

However you wash the car, use the opportunity to check the paintwork for scratches and stone chips. If the scratch or chip is deep enough, rust may get under the paint. As a short-term measure, make sure the scratch or chip is clean and dry, and then smear it liberally with petroleum jelly. Deep scratches and chips should be dealt with properly. If you can get a 'touch-up' paint kit that matches (car accessory shops stock them), clean the damage with a drop of methylated spirits on a clean, lint-free rag before applying the paint very delicately with a tiny brush. Don't be tempted to spray or paint indiscriminately or your car will look as though it has measles, and need professional respraying.

Interior

A quick vacuum through the interior, at the same time mucking out the sweet papers and parking tickets and shaking the mats, will make the car a more pleasant place to be in, and help to improve its value when the time comes to sell. In today's motoring environment dirt gets everywhere. Even if a cigarette has never been inside your car, the insides of the windows will be dirty – particularly the front screen, which gets the muck coming in from the air vents. Rub your finger across it and see. You can clean it with commercial window cleaner, but you can also buy wipes designed for the job in resealable packs. A regular wipe with one of these will keep the screen clear. Similar products for the outside of the screen clear it of diesel film, dead insects and bird droppings.

Don't allow people to smoke in the car. The smell pervades the upholstery and will linger for ever. Non-smokers are less likely to buy a car which has been inhabited by smokers. You can use air fresheners, but most of them smell almost as bad. If you carry **pets** in the car, put them in a box or on an old blanket. Dog hairs cling tenaciously to some modern upholstery fabrics.

THE MoT TEST

All cars over three years old have to undergo an annual check to ensure that they comply with basic safety and legal requirements. Without a current test certificate you won't be able to tax or insure the car, and failure to have one could mean a £1,000 fine. The test costs approximately £24 and can be carried out at any authorised test centre you choose. Test centres – usually, but not always, garages – display a blue and white sign.

The tester will examine the car's brakes, steering, wheel bearings, suspension, shock absorbers, wheels, tyres and exhaust system. The emissions from the exhaust are also tested, as are the fuel tank and fuel pipes.

The seat mountings and the seat belts are tested, as are the horn, windscreen wipers and washers. The tester will examine the bodywork, windscreen, mirrors (which must be undamaged) and look to see that the driver's view is unobstructed. So anything hanging from the mirror, or mounted on the rear parcel shelf, must be removed together with stickers other than essential ones. Away with nodding dogs whose eyes blink when you brake, and furry dice dangling from the rear-view mirror.

The test sounds comprehensive, but just because a car has a valid MoT certificate, it does not mean that nothing will go wrong with it, in the same way that a doctor cannot guarantee that you will not have a heart attack on the day after a medical.

About one car in four fails the test. If yours does, the tester will tell you what needs to be done to remedy the defects. You need not have the car repaired at the garage where the test was done, and you can drive home or to another garage without a current test certificate. It is wisest to have a car tested a couple of weeks before you need a certificate, in case it needs treatment.

17. Security

Your car is a very expensive purchase and it is up to you to keep it safe. Car crime is a booming business. There are 2 million thefts of or from cars every year and the figure is rising. Although you will never prevent determined professional thieves from taking your car or its contents if that is what they want, you can reduce the odds enormously by taking precautions.

LOCK THE CAR

It may sound obvious, but remember to lock all the car doors plus the boot, and close the windows every time you leave the car. One in five cars parked on the street is left unlocked or with its windows open. Never leave a child or an animal alone in a car. They do not deter thieves and could come to harm.

ENGAGE THE STEERING COLUMN LOCK

Unless your car is very old it will be fitted with a steering lock, which you activate by turning the steering wheel when the car is parked and the ignition key removed. The lock is engaged when the steering wheel will not move, and this makes the car difficult to steal. Turning the key in the ignition unlocks the steering column, although you may need to wiggle the wheel a bit at the same time.

REMOVE TEMPTATION

Do not leave anything in the car that might attract thieves. If you cannot take it with you put shopping, luggage, coats, tapes etc. out of sight in the boot and lock it. This is particularly important at Christmas and holiday time.

Don't keep vehicle documents in the car. And take car park tickets with you unless you are in a 'pay and display' area.

RADIO/CASSETTE/DISC PLAYER

These are a favourite target for thieves. If yours is removable, take it with you. Only lock it in the boot if there is no alternative. Some car radios are coded so that they will not work outside the car in which they are installed and a warning sticker on the car window may deter professional thieves. Or you can mark the radio with the car's registration number.

WINDOW ETCHING

If it has not already been done when the car is new, have the registration number or VIN (see Glossary) etched on to the windows. A car thief will not be keen to replace all the windows as well as the number plates. Most garages will do window etching, or the Crime Prevention Officer at your local police station should have a list of specialist companies. You can buy a kit and do it yourself.

CAR ALARMS

Have an alarm system fitted, preferably one that incorporates an immobiliser and flashing warning lights. Display the sticker which shows what security precautions you have taken.

There are dozens of car alarms on the market, and they vary considerably in price. If you are buying a new car it is best to choose one of the alarms which the manufacturer fits when the car is built. Some models have alarm systems fitted as standard equipment, often the key-switch variety, in which the doors, bonnet and boot are fitted with contact breakers so that when any of these are forced open, the alarm sounds. It doesn't stop thieves smashing a window, but they are unlikely to climb into the car with an alarm going. Ultrasonic alarms work by covering the inside of the car with electronic waves, which trigger the alarm when they are disturbed by a window smashing or someone getting into the car. But unless they have a sensitivity control they can be triggered by draughts, or extremes of temperature. Microwave alarm systems are more expensive but less volatile and less likely to disturb the neighbours by going off accidentally.

At the top of the range are the systems which also disable the electrics and prevent the car starting. Some systems incorporate a panic button, which operates the alarm from the driver's seat if you want to summon help. Whichever system you choose, try to have a flashing light visible from outside the car when the alarm is set. There are so many cars without alarms that an opportunist thief will probably move on to one of those. Of course, the truly professional thief who has set his sights on your expensive car can lift it on to a low-loader and drive away. There isn't much you can do about that.

SIMPLE ANTI-THEFT DEVICES

If your car is old, you are unlikely to want to spend hundreds of pounds on an elaborate alarm system. Mechanical devices that stop the steering wheel being turned, or the gear level moved, won't stop anyone breaking into the car, but they might make a thief think twice about stealing it. Garage forecourt shops and car accessory shops stock them. Nothing is thief-proof, but anything that takes time to unravel will buy you some security.

A locking filler cap means that thieves will not easily be able to fill up with petrol when the tank runs dry, and if they are planning a long journey they may prefer someone else's car. Nor will it be easy for anyone to drain your tank if they find themselves out of petrol.

If your car has expensive and covetable alloy wheels, fit locking wheel nuts. Again, experienced thieves will remove them in a matter of minutes but they might be put off if your car is parked somewhere conspicuous.

VEHICLE WATCH

This is a free scheme in which several police forces participate, particularly in the London area. When you register with your local police station you will be given two stickers, which are put on the windscreen and rear window of your vehicle by the police. They do not come off easily. If you rarely, if ever, use your car between 12.30 a.m. and 5.00 a.m., you fix the yellow sticker to the rear window. If a police officer sees the car being driven during that period, he or she will know that it shouldn't be on the road and will stop the vehicle, question the occupant and take the appropriate action. The daytime scheme (10 a.m.–4.30 p.m.) uses the orange sticker.

GARAGE
If you have a garage, use it.

WHAT TO DO IF YOUR CAR IS STOLEN
If your car is not where you left it, phone the police. An astonishing number of people report their car stolen when they have simply forgotten where they parked. This often happens in multi-storey car parks, and in areas where all the streets look alike. As well as memorising or writing down your vehicle registration number, make a note of the street or car park space where you have parked.

The car may have been towed away, not stolen. The police will want to know the make, model, colour and registration number of the vehicle, where you left it and when you last saw it. If it has been towed away, it will cost you approximately £100 to retrieve it.

If the car has been stolen, your insurance policy requires you to get in touch with your insurance company. Do this as soon as possible. Most companies will not pay out on a stolen car for some months, so check whether your insurance pays for you to hire a car. Even if it does, it won't be for more than a few days.

A Fiat poster in 1979 showed a 127 Palio. It bore the line 'If it were a lady, it would get its bottom pinched.' Graffiti artists added: 'If this lady were a car, she'd run you down.'

18. Children in Cars

The effect of the head of a small child hitting the windscreen of a car travelling at 30m.p.h. is the equivalent of dropping the child 30 feet out of a window on to a pavement.

Cars are not a natural habitat for children of any age, although some small babies find it very soothing to be driven around. But the wide range of safety seats and harnesses available today means that children can be safe and comfortable passengers. Children cannot protect themselves. *The responsibility for their safety is that of drivers, whether they are the parents or not.*

➤ How many children do you carry in your car?
➤ Have they all got suitable safety restraints?
➤ Do you do a school run?

SEATS AND SEAT BELTS

Every child in a car should have their own seat and seat belt. That isn't just the law – it's common sense. The safest place is in the back seat where adult seat belts can be used to anchor child seats or carrycots. Unlike most European countries, the UK still allows children to be carried in the front passenger seat, and over the age of 4 they need only use an adult seat-belt. But there are large 4-year-olds and small 4-year-olds and making distinctions by age rather than by size and weight is clearly silly. In a crash, a small child wearing an adult seat belt is liable to slither out from under it (known as submarining). It is extraordinary that the position in a car which for years was known as 'the suicide seat' because its occupant was most likely to be hurt in an accident, is the one in which we allow our children to travel with least protection.

As well as child seats, small babies can be carried in a carrycot restrained on the back seat, but this is less satisfactory than a properly fitted car seat. It is legal to use a carrycot with special restraints, but remember that it is the carrycot which is restrained, not the baby, and if the car were to roll over, the baby could be thrown out. Many parents prefer to have the baby seat fitted in the front passenger seat facing backwards so that they can keep an eye on the baby while driving, and indeed many manufacturers suggest this. But legislation is on the way which will make it mandatory to carry all children in the back seat. If you have a new car fitted with a safety air bag (see Glossary) on the passenger side, the baby or child seat should definitely be in the back. The back seat is always safer, if less convenient.

> 'Casabianca, Robin and Vicky, with better feeling, push car vigorously, and eventually get it into the lane, when engine starts again. Quarter of a mile further on, Felicity informs me that she thinks one of the children is hanging on to the back of the car. I stop, investigate and discover Robin, to whom I speak severely. He looks abashed. I relent, and say, Well, never mind this time, at which he recovers immediately, and waves us off with many smiles from the top of the hedge'
>
> From the novel *The Diary of a Provincial Lady* by E. M. Delafield' (Virago)

Increasingly, maternity units do not let a newborn baby leave hospital in a car unless the child is properly restrained in a baby seat. Some hospitals will rent or loan seats, but it is best to be prepared.

When children have outgrown their safety seats, which can be at any age from 4 to 7 depending on their height, they may graduate

to adult belts used with a booster cushion. This lifts the child up so that the belt fits safely round them, and has the added advantage of letting them see out of the window.

The temptation to put too many children in a car, especially on a school run or a birthday trip, is enormous. But each model is designed for a specific number of people (usually five) and if you overload it, some passengers will not be wearing seat belts. If you have an accident, not only may the cost be enormous in terms of suffering, but the insurance company could refuse a claim. Even if you do not have an accident, you can be fined up to £1,000 and have your licence endorsed if you fail to carry passengers safely.

There is as yet no law preventing children travelling loose in the luggage compartment of an estate car or hatchback, but it is dangerous. Proper rear-facing seats with seat belts in the luggage space of an estate car provide the only safe solution.

Children unrestrained in cars can have accidents all by themselves. Childproof locks are fitted on rear doors so that if a child opens the door it cannot fall out, but they need to be set. Some electric window systems and cigarette lighters work even if the ignition is switched off. *Think very hard before you leave children alone in a car. And NEVER leave the ignition keys in*.

LONG JOURNEYS

Travelling alone with children on long journeys can be purgatory. Even if it prolongs the journey, plan more breaks than usual. Make the children as comfortable as possible and put toys within reach. See that they have adequate ventilation. It is better to wrap them up and have fresh air than to overheat the car. Avoid too much fluid and sweet things before and during the journey and in the summer check that the children are not getting overheated in the sun. A stick-on driving mirror angled on to the back seat lets you see what the children are up to without having to turn round. Tape players with story tapes are a useful diversion as are pencils and paper but if you are the only adult stick to simple games like I-spy which are not too distracting for you.

If you are travelling long distances in winter with babies or small children, carry an emergency kit of blanket/duvet, drink and some food, in case you get stuck and have to wait some time for help.

Despite your best efforts, some children get car-sick, often because they have been reading or the car is stuffy. They usually grow out of it, but it can be distressing for them and disgusting for everyone else. Essential equipment includes a roll of kitchen paper, wipes, a bottle of plain water and sick-bags. The highest-quality sick-bags come from car ferries and aircraft, but if you haven't been able to collect any, a stout brown paper bag lined with a plastic bag makes a good substitute. Children being sick is *not* seen by the police as a good reason for stopping on a motorway.

19. Special Drivers

THE PREGNANT DRIVER

There is no reason why a pregnant woman should not drive, unless her medical advisers warn against it. Every adult in a car must wear a seat belt, and so must a pregnant woman. It protects both the woman and the unborn child in the event of an accident. Pregnancy does not exempt you from the law.

It is worth taking a minute or two to adjust the seat and belt. The buckle should be low down against the thigh, the shoulder strap between the breasts and the lap strap under the bulge. Modern automatic seat belts will expand as you do and many have an adjustment on the door pillar which raises or lowers the diagonal belt. Because women in the later stages of pregnancy often need to go to the loo, plan frequent stops. Swollen ankles can make driving long distances uncomfortable, and discomfort affects concentration, so be prepared and do not attempt to drive too long without a break.

It is very important that a pregnant woman travelling as a passenger in the back seat should be comfortably restrained by a seat belt. In an accident a pregnant woman without a seat belt can cannon into the front seat and cause serious injuries to herself, the unborn baby and the front-seat passenger.

After the birth some doctors advise women not to drive until after their post-natal check – usually about six weeks. This may seem unnecessary in many cases but after a birth by Caesarean section, or one involving total anaesthetic, it is good advice and should be heeded. Drivers need to be alert, and childbirth is a tiring business.

If you have to call an emergency service on an ordinary road or motorway, remember to tell the operator that you are a pregnant woman, so that you can get priority help.

Women drivers have been the butt of many a motoring joke. In their book, *How To Be a Motorist*, first published in 1936, Heath Robinson and K.R.G. Browne give serious advice to road users. 'It is dashed bad form to overtake a blonde fellow-motorist on a blind corner, or to cut-in on her in such a way as to edge her into a ditch. Cars wearing large crimson 'Ls' and driven, more or less by typical English women, should be treated with profound respect, as nobody – least of all, as a rule, the typical Englishwoman – can foretell what they are likely to do next. In fact, and to beat about no more bushes, the male motorist's attitude towards she-drivers of all ages should be one of flawless but rather distant courtesy, tinged slightly with apprehension.'

THE MATURE DRIVER

Older people are more active and mobile than ever before but they may find that their sight, hearing and judgement of speed and distance are not as sharp as they were. Nevertheless, the car is just as liberating for the older woman driver as for the younger, even if it is only used for short journeys – to go to the shops or meet friends – and often widows find that to drive a car is to maintain a vital link with the outside world.

The number of older people is increasing, representing a significant proportion of the population in the UK. Today the proportion of drivers over 65 years old is more than 15 per cent. Given common sense and good health, there is no reason why an older woman should not continue to drive for many years.

- ▶ How long is it since you saw your doctor and told him or her that you drive?
- ▶ How long is it since you saw an optician and told him or her the same thing?
- ▶ Is your car regularly serviced?
- ▶ Are you a member of a breakdown service?

Current driving licences expire when the driver is 70. Every three years after that, drivers must renew their licences, yet they only have to fill in the same form as that given to drivers applying for their first licence. But older people suffer deterioration of eyesight and increasing health problems, and the onus is on the driver to be honest when filling in the form. The 'patient's charter' now requires doctors to see every elderly patient regularly, although there is no similar requirement for a driver's eyes to be tested. Very occasionally a doctor or consultant will get in touch with the DVLA (Driver and Vehicle Licensing Agency) in Swansea to say that a driver should not have a licence, but generally the driver has to be honest and realistic.

To feel safe as an older driver it is wise to be checked by both a doctor and an optician on a regular basis. But it is equally important to drive a car that is right for your needs. A smaller car, perhaps with automatic transmission and certainly with power steering, may be more suitable than the car you have. It is important for an older driver to have a car that is reliable: an elderly driver will not want to change a wheel or wait in the cold for help. A well-maintained car and membership of a motoring organisation are essential.

THE DISABLED DRIVER

If a car provides independence for the able-bodied, it can do much more for the disabled. For many disabled people the car is the most convenient and flexible method of transport.

Various things make life easier for disabled drivers: among them the government-sponsored Motability, the Disabled Living Allowance, the Orange Badge scheme, the Disabled Drivers' Association, the Disabled Motorists' Federation and the Banstead Mobility Centre (part of the Queen Elizabeth Foundation for the Disabled), which provides a comprehensive service for disabled people who want to drive, or be a passenger in a vehicle suited to their particular needs (see Address Book).

But just as important are the things which other motorists can do to make the disabled motorist's life easier.

▶ Do not park in a space designated for disabled drivers.
▶ Do not park so close to a car displaying an Orange Badge that a disabled person, perhaps in a wheelchair, cannot get into the car.
▶ If you see a stranded motorist displaying a 'Help: disabled' notice, please stop to see what you can do. Unlike other drivers, the disabled driver may not be able to get to an emergency telephone and may need urgent assistance.

Helpline

The AA has a free telephone information helpline for the disabled, providing advice and information on all aspects of mobility for disabled motorists. Helpline can also be used by disabled AA members to obtain priority roadside service.

Deaf or hard-of-hearing motorists can buy Minicom, an AA communication system used with a telephone. When a deaf driver needs breakdown assistance they dial the emergency number which alerts AA staff. The AA operator types a message to the caller asking for details and the driver can reply.

20. Motoring and the Law

PENALTY POINTS

On the assumption that you have taken and passed a driving test in the UK, you will have some idea of motoring law. The details change from time to time, but the principles remain the same.

Your driving licence allows you 12 penalty points. Every time you are convicted of a motoring offence, points will be recorded on the licence. Any driver who accumulates 12 or more points within a three-year period must be disqualified for a minimum of six months. If this happens, you will find that getting insurance when you get your licence back will be more expensive, if not impossible. The new *Highway Code* lists the most frequent offences and the penalties they are likely to attract.

MOTORING OFFENCES

Speeding and drink/drive are the two offences most commonly committed and convictions for both are becoming increasingly severe as the government moves to reduce Britain's 5,000 road deaths a year.

If you are convicted of a motoring offence, penalty points will be recorded on your licence and the fine will be judged according to your disposable income. The more you earn, the more you pay. Penalties can be anything from a few hundred pounds to a custodial sentence, depending on the gravity of your offence and your financial status. A speeding conviction usually attracts 3–6 penalty points and the maximum fine for a speeding offence on a motorway is £2,500. Courts can also order a convicted driver to retake a driving test. For a driver convicted of dangerous driving, or of causing death by dangerous driving, the retest will be twice as long as the ordinary test.

> A traffic problem existed in the narrow streets of pre-revolutionary Paris. It was customary for society ladies of the time to drive their own carriages and not even King Louis XVI dared risk their displeasure by forbidding them to drive. One of the king's senior ministers, Count d'Argenson, was asked if he would unsnarl the traffic jams diplomatically. 'Of course,' replied d'Argenson. I will simply pass this law: Ladies under 30 years of age are forbidden to drive carriages.'

Although there is a legal limit for the amount of alcohol a driver may have in his or her blood without committing an offence (a breath alcohol level of 35 mg per 100 ml, equivalent to a blood alcohol level of 80 mg per 100 ml) there is absolutely no foolproof way of knowing whether you are over the limit, until you are tested by a police breathalyser.

The only safe course is not to drink *anything* alcoholic if you are planning to drive. Women – because their body weight is usually less that of the equivalent male – can reach the legal limit very quickly, and it simply isn't worth the risk. You can be imprisoned, disqualified and/or heavily fined. Drink/drive rehabilitation courses are to be started in some courts.

Drivers convicted of drinking and driving twice within ten years – if they are two and a half times over the legal limit, or if they refuse to give a blood or urine specimen – will also have to satisfy the DVLA's medical branch that they do not have an alcohol problem before they get their licence back.

The new way of catching a speeding motorist is by roadside camera (known as **Gatso**). These cameras photograph the rear number plate of a speeding car at the same time as a panel displaying the time of day and the speed of the car. Even if you have seen the warning signs, you will only know that you have been caught

when the summons drops through the letterbox. Unlike some other devices, the Gatso is considered reliable, so there is no defence against it. Speeding penalties are a fine of up to £1,000, a discretionary ban and up to 6 penalty points. So in theory you could lose your licence in a mile and two minutes.

There are cameras which spot drivers who jump the lights. These are also accepted by the courts as incontrovertible evidence. Even if you tell the police that someone else was driving the car you can be fined £1,000 and 3 penalty points for not telling them who it was.

Recent changes to the Road Traffic Act mean that you can be prosecuted for bad driving and drink-driving in a supermarket car park, on private roads and waste land, as well as on public highways.

21. Motoring Abroad

One of the great joys of motoring is to be able to explore, at home and abroad. 'Abroad' often means driving on the other side of the road, but with care and concentration this is not difficult.

PLANNING

If you are planning to drive abroad, think ahead. Every country has different demands in terms of what motorists should carry in their cars and you must be aware of them. For example, in Switzerland you must have a spare pair of spectacles if you use them for driving, in Germany a first-aid kit, in France you must be carrying your driving licence and the Italians don't allow a spare can of fuel in the car. The motoring organisations can be of great help: they have all the necessary information and will advise you. You can also hire touring kits of spares for your trip.

If your car uses unleaded fuel, make a note of the name used for it in the countries where you plan to drive. Unleaded petrol is still difficult to find in Portugal and Turkey.

Not all petrol stations take credit cards, especially in Italy. Austrian petrol stations never do. And although most French traffic police will take a credit card to pay for a fine, you cannot be certain. Have sufficient cash with you for motorway tolls, and for emergencies.

DO NOT GO ABROAD WITHOUT IT. Although your normal car insurance will be legal in EC countries, you should take out extra insurance, usually called a 'green card'. Very often personal injury awards made by continental countries are well in excess of anything your UK insurance will cover you for. Consult your insurance company or a motoring organisation. You should also make sure that you have adequate medical insurance. If you are going to the EC, the British National Health Service has a reciprocal agreement with other member states' medical services; your local Department of Health office will provide the appropriate form, which you must complete before you leave. Some countries demand money up front for medical treatment and refund it afterwards.

If you are going to the US on a fly-drive holiday, make insurance arrangements before you leave. That way you can make certain that you are insured for all eventualities, which may not be the case if you take out *ad hoc* insurance in America.

BREAKDOWNS

Your insurance paperwork should indicate what to do in the event of a breakdown or an accident. Many companies that specialise in motor insurance have 24-hour lines with multilingual operators so that even if you cannot communicate with local people, you can call and get help. This can be vital if you have a medical problem. Make sure that you have all the necessary phone numbers before you leave home.

MOTORING LAWS

These also vary from country to country. You should be aware of laws concerning speed limits, regulations about children in cars, drink/drive and parking, most of which are more stringent abroad than they are here. Some countries are very fierce about the way in which they treat drivers who infringe their laws.

Some laws are unexpected – for example, you can be fined on the spot for running out of petrol on a German autobahn (motorway), and being rude to policemen, and in Russia it is illegal to drive a dirty car.

International driving licences, which are obtainable from motoring organisations, give your details in several languages. It is illegal to drive with one of these if you have not got a valid licence in your country of residence, but some countries expect you to carry one. If you are successfully prosecuted for a motoring offence in an EC country, you can expect the fact to be reported to the British authorities.

> Dorothy Levitt advised women in 1909: 'Ladies are usually bad at judging distances, and it is well to keep as much toward the middle of the road as possible'

DRIVING ON THE 'WRONG' SIDE OF THE ROAD

If you have never driven on the right-hand side of the road, take it carefully to start with. If you are driving your British car, the steering wheel is closest to the kerb. This makes it difficult to overtake. A front-seat passenger can help by letting you know when the road ahead is clear, so work out a code so that there cannot be any misunderstanding. If you are driving alone, you can sometimes see round the *inside* of the vehicle in front of you.

Driving a car with the steering wheel on the left is very easy. The pedals are exactly the same as they are on a UK car. You will operate the gear lever with your right hand (first gear will be nearest to you and top gear furthest away), and you will be able to overtake as you do in the UK.

You are most likely to get confused when you set off from a car park, petrol station or at a roundabout. Some people find that it helps to stick a little bit of coloured paper on the right-hand corner of the screen, to help them remember that it is that side of the car which should be closest to the kerb.

LIGHTS

Headlights on right-hand-drive cars are set so that when they are dipped, the oncoming driver is not dazzled. Most handbooks show you how to modify them with a piece of opaque tape, but if you have a problem, ask a motoring organisation. Their representatives at the channel ports are extremely helpful.

It is no longer necessary to have amber headlights when you drive in France. These were introduced during the war to make it easy to distinguish between domestic and foreign vehicles.

Equip yourself with maps and guides before you leave Britain, and check when you buy them that they are up to date. Road systems change so rapidly that a five-year-old map could leave you very puzzled.

22. Motoring and the Environment

The purists will tell you that there is nothing environmentally sound about the car. But 'environment' should be viewed in the round, and for many people using a car is the only way in which they can remain mobile – not any longer by choice but by necessity.

The automotive industry has become an essential feature of world economy. But combine the need for mobility with the need for economic growth, and you have a car park which is growing at about 19 million cars a year worldwide. Necessary though the car industry may be, it is also clear that we must think about the problem this poses for the environment.

If there is not exactly a 'green revolution' in motoring, there is increasing 'green awareness'. Governments are beginning to legislate against pollution, manufacturers are researching ways of reducing fuel consumption, and there is a worldwide trend towards effective public transport systems. But while we wait for a transport nirvana, we drive cars. So what can a driver do to lessen the impact of the car on today's environment?

► Drive a car which is as small as possible for the journeys you make and the things or people you need to carry.
► Buy a car which is fitted with a catalytic converter and runs on unleaded fuel or diesel.

▶ Have the car serviced and tuned regularly.
▶ Restrict your speed.
▶ Adjust your driving style so that you can drive smoothly and with anticipation.
▶ Leave the car at home as often as possible.

DRIVING FOR THE ENVIRONMENT

If you drive as though you have eggs between your feet and the pedals, you will have made an important step towards driving for the environment. Fierce use of the controls increases fuel consumption and increases stress on both the car and you. Gentle acceleration and braking, and driving in as high a gear as sounds comfortable, is 'green' driving.

RECYCLING

Ironically, one of the least environmental aspects of the car is what happens to it when it's finished. Scrap-heaps of rotting vehicles are to be found all over the world because recycling is a concept new to the motor industry. German manufacturers gave a lead in building cars which are designed for ultimate recycling. Already recycling plants are appearing in Britain which will dismantle old cars, and process their components. Until these become commonplace there are only a couple of things the car owner can do to protect the environment.

If you change the oil in your car (not difficult, but a bit messy), you are faced with the problem of getting rid of the old oil. If you illegally pour used oil down a drain, over the ground, or even put it into your dustbin, it will eventually find its way into the water system and destroy the natural food chain. Your local authority should have a disposal point, or at least be able to tell you where to find one.

If you have an old battery, it should not be left to rot. If your local authority has no way of getting rid of it, any BMW dealer will take old car batteries from any make of car.

STARTING UP

There is a motoring myth which says that you should start the car and then let it idle (stand with the engine running) for some time before moving off. Do not do this.

As soon as you have started the engine, drive away. Letting the engine run while you defrost the windows and warm up the seat wastes fuel through the exhaust and leaves noxious emissions in the air. When you are ready to go, start up and accelerate gently. Make sure you have cleared the window of frost beforehand.

CAR SHARING

Too many cars on the roads have only one occupant. Many people value the solitude which being alone in a car gives them, but the environment suffers. If there is someone whom you know well and who makes the same daily journey as you, consider sharing a car rather than taking one each. This does *not* mean picking someone up at the bus stop, or giving a lift to a stranger, neither of which is safe. But properly organised, car sharing is environmentally friendly.

OTHER ROAD USERS

Not everyone has a car. Pedestrians, cyclists and horse riders have just as much right to mobility as motorists, but the car is able to inflict substantial damage both to other road users and to the environment.

Be considerate. If you show respect for other road users, you will make a small but long-term contribution to integrated transport. By law, a cyclist is entitled to wobble. Leave a bicycle plenty of space – the seconds you save by scraping past are insignificant in the general scheme of things.

Pedestrians come in all shapes, sizes and states of health. From the driving seat you cannot tell whether the person crossing the road in front of you is deaf, disabled or drunk. Give every pedestrian the benefit of the doubt. You may be in a hurry, but at least you are warm and dry.

CHILDREN AS PEDESTRIANS

Children, whether on feet or wheels, are unreliable road users. If you are driving in an area where there are likely to be children – for example around schools or in housing estates – keep your wits about you.

If you are a parent it is essential that you supervise your children on the road. There is a great temptation, as well as pressure from the children themselves, to let them on to the road alone. At the risk of making yourself deeply unpopular, supervise every child on the road.

FOUR-WHEEL DRIVING IN THE COUNTRY

Most four-wheel-drive (4WD) vehicles never climb anything higher than the kerb. But a modern 4WD vehicle can take you all over the country: you can explore parts of the landscape inaccessible to drivers of ordinary cars.

But although off-road driving is fun, you can easily destroy the countryside. *Slow and safe* is the golden rule. If you fancy serious off-road driving, take a course at a specialist school before you set off. Otherwise you could find yourself in serious difficulties.

HORSES

Horses do not read the *Highway Code*, and the fact that they usually live in the country means that they are not accustomed to the unexpected. Cars and horses do not mix, so if you come across a horse on the road, assume that it is nervous. Don't hoot, change to a low gear and drive slowly until the rider gives you a sign to pass.

> The role of women in motoring at the turn of the century was strictly passive. Here is the Hon. John Scott-Montagu, writing in *The Utility of Motor Vehicles*:
>
> 'For fetching guests from the station in the country, I would recommend a covered as well as an open motor, or perhaps a motor which can have a top fitted when the weather is bad. Ladies do not like arriving at teatime with their fringes out of curl or the feathers of their hats drooping or facing the wrong way'

23. Selling your Car

If you want to sell your car, rather than part-exchange it for a new one, you will probably get the best price by advertising it privately. But it is a tedious business, so if the car is newish and in good condition, start by offering it to a few garages – ideally those which specialise in the make. This will give you some idea of what the trade price is likely to be.

By looking at car small-ads in the national press, car magazines and *Exchange & Mart* you will also get a good idea of current prices. Build in a good margin so that you can reduce the price when bargaining.

- ▶ Is the car in good condition?
- ▶ Have you got a sensible price in mind?
- ▶ Have you got all the paperwork?

When you concoct the advertisement, keep it short and to the point, with only a telephone number – no name. Do not see prospective customers alone – always have someone with you, especially in the car during a test-drive and if you invite them into the house to conclude a deal.

It isn't wise to leave a prospective buyer alone in the car with the keys. Ask him or her if they are insured before you let them drive the car.

In the 1950s, it was still rare for a car to be advertised with a woman at the wheel. An exception was the Daimler Conquest convertible, which featured a folding hood, mechanically operated at the touch of a button. Whilst the main picture shows a woman in the driving seat pressing the button which operates the hood, in smaller drawings also on the advert, men are at the wheel.

Have the paperwork ready – log book, service book, MoT and as many bills for repairs and maintenance as you can find.

Even if you have priced the car too low, your potential buyer will haggle. Unless you are desperate, don't be persuaded to go below the lowest price you have in your head. If the buyer offers cash, all well and good. But if the buyer offers you a bank cheque or a building society cheque, make sure it has been cleared before you part with the car. Banks offer a special clearing facility, for which they charge. *Never part with the car until the cheque has been cleared or you have the cash in your hand*. Treat even certified building society cheques and bankers' drafts with caution. A phone call to verify them may save you a lot of heartache.

Make out an invoice – with a copy – and make the customer sign them both. You must fill out the transfer section of the registration document yourself, or you may find yourself getting someone else's speeding fines.

If the car is a bit tatty or long in the tooth, or you are getting no joy from the small-ads, you could try to sell at auction. If there is a local car auction, find out on which day they sell and how the system works. Then get the car there in plenty of time. Give it a good clean, inside and out. You can put a reserve price on it.

Putting a 'For Sale' sign in the car window isn't recommended. It rarely works, and may get you unwanted attention.

24. For Northern Ireland Motorists

There are several differences in motoring legislation between Great Britain and Northern Ireland.

HIGHWAY CODE

In most practical terms the NI and GB highway codes are the same but with some important exceptions:

▶ a newly qualified driver must display an 'R-plate' on the front and rear of the vehicle for 12 months after passing the test.
▶ 'R' drivers may not exceed a speed of 45m.p.h. Speed limits of 30m.p.h. and 40m.p.h. must, of course, be obeyed.
▶ in NI the headlights of cars have to be on between the hours of sunset and sunrise. In GB sidelights only are required in well-lit, built-up areas.

DRIVING TEST

▶ In NI, examinees are required to produce a driving licence showing that they are licensed to drive, whereas in GB only some form of identification is required.
▶ in NI the first MoT test takes place after 5 years, not 3 as in GB.
▶ an MoT test can only be carried out in authorised test centres (not at garage centres as in GB).

Glossary

ABS   *A*nti-lock *B*raking *S*ystem, which prevents wheels locking.

AIR BAG   Passenger restraint system using a bag concealed in front of the driver and front seat passenger, which inflates in milliseconds if the car crashes, to prevent the head and chest hitting the steering wheel or facia.

AIR LINE   Sources of compressed air for inflating tyres found on garage forecourts.

ALIGNMENT   The adjustment of suspension and steering so that the wheels point straight ahead when the car is running in a straight line.

ALTERNATOR   The generator in a modern car which produces electric current.

ANTIFREEZE   Liquid added to the car's cooling system to prevent it freezing.

ANTI-ROLL BAR   A U-shaped rod which is linked at both ends to the axle or suspension and helps to resist body roll.

APR   *A*nnual *P*ercentage *R*ate, as used in loans and hire purchase agreements.

AUTOMATIC TRANSMISSION   Gearbox without a foot-operated clutch.

BOOSTER CUSHION   A firm pad which lifts a child so that the seat belt fits correctly.

BULKHEAD   That part of the car's bodywork which separates the engine compartment from the passenger compartment.

BUMP-START   Starting the engine by letting the car roll down a slope or having the car pushed, and then engaging the clutch when the car is moving.

CATALYTIC CONVERTER   Device used in the exhaust system, which uses precious metals to reduce the concentration of noxious gases that would otherwise be released into the atmosphere.

CENTRAL LOCKING   Device which locks all the car doors by locking one front door.

CHILDPROOF LOCKS   Locks which prevent the rear passenger doors being opened from the inside. Usually found on the edge of the doors. See handbook.

DAMPER   Also called **shock absorber**. Used in the suspension to stop the springs from 'bouncing' after passing over a bump in the road.

DERV   Another name for diesel fuel (diesel engined road vehicle).

DISTILLED WATER   Water from which impurities have been removed. Best used to refill batteries. Can be bought in garages and car accessory shops.

EMERGENCY TRIANGLE   A free-standing, collapsible, fluorescent triangle carried in the boot. Place about 50m behind a car which has broken down, to warn other road users.

FACIA   Another name for **dashboard**.

FOUR-WHEEL DRIVE   Vehicle in which all four wheels are driven by the engine, instead of just the front wheels or the rear wheels.

GATSO   Camera which records speeding motorists.

GRILLE   The panel in front of the radiator which allows air to pass through when the car is moving.

HEADER TANK   The upper tank of the radiator, which has a pressurising filler cap. On sealed cooling systems the pressure cap is on an overflow tank.

JACK   Device for raising the car in order to change a wheel. Provided with the car when new. See handbook.

JACKING POINTS   Places where the car's jack must be placed. See handbook.

JUMP LEADS   Cables (red and black), with bulldog clips on each end, which are used to start an engine with a flat battery by feeding current from a donor battery.

MASTER CYLINDER   A reservoir with a screw cap, which acts as a pump for the hydraulic system.

MoT   The test necessary for a car more than three years old. Must be carried out by a test centre authorised by the Department of Transport.

POWER-ASSISTED   Used to describe a mechanism that reduces the effort needed by the driver to brake or steer.

REGISTRATION DOCUMENT   (Often called 'log-book'.) The document which comes with a new vehicle, listing its make, model and details. Names of owners are also listed.

SILL   The part of a car's bodywork below the door, between the front and rear wheel arches.

SLEEPING POLICEMEN   Humps in the road to deter speeding drivers.

STARTER MOTOR   Motor which turns the engine when the ignition key is turned.

STEERING ARM   Connects steering wheel to the wheels. Usually visible under the car. *Not* substantial enough for towing.

TAIL PIPE   The part of the exhaust system that protrudes from beneath the car.

TERMINAL   Part of the battery to which a jump lead can be attached.

THERMOSTAT   A device for regulating the temperature of the car's cooling system.

TRIM   Word used to describe the fittings of the car's interior.

TRIP METER   Counter on facia which records miles driven. Can be put to zero at touch of a button. See handbook.

TURBO-CHARGER   A small turbine driven by the engine's exhaust gases, which drives a compressor to force air into the engine to give increased performance and fuel economy, while keeping the engine size small.

TYRE PRESSURE   The pressure to which a tyre must be inflated to support the weight of the car while affording optimum ride comfort, handling and grip.

TYRE TREAD   The rubber outer layer of a tyre, carrying the tread pattern which clears water from wet surfaces.

UNLEADED PETROL   Petrol to which no health-damaging lead has been added. Usually dispensed from pumps with green hoses. Must be used in cars fitted with catalytic converters.

VIN   *V*ehicle *I*dentification *N*umber.

WARNING LIGHT   Light on the facia to alert the driver to a malfunction.

WATER REPELLENT   A spray used to dry out a damp engine.

Address book

ABI (Association of British Insurers; for motor insurance problems)

Aldermary House
Queen Street
London EC4N 1TT
Tel: 071 248 4477

AUTOMOBILE ASSOCIATION

Fanum House
Basingstoke
Hants RG21 EA
Tel: 0256 20123
Disability Helpline:
0800 262050

BANSTEAD MOBILITY CENTRE

Damson Way
Orchard Hill
Queen Mary's Avenue
Carshalton
Surrey SM5 4NR
Tel: 081 770 1151

THE CARAVAN CLUB

East Grinstead House
East Grinstead
West Sussex RH19 1UA
Tel: 0342 326944

CENTRAL MOTOR AUCTIONS

Central House
Pontefract Road
Rothwell
Leeds LS26 0JE
Tel: 0532 820707

CITIZENS ADVICE BUREAU

See local telephone directory

CONSUMERS' ASSOCIATION

2 Marylebone Road
London NW1 4DX
Tel: 071 486 5544

DEPARTMENT OF TRANSPORT	2 Marsham Street London SW1P 3EB Tel: 071 276 3000
DISABLED DRIVERS' ASSOCIATION	The Hall Ashwellthorpe Norwich Norfolk NR16 1EX Tel: 050 841 449
DISABLED MOTORISTS' FEDERATION	The National Mobility Centre Unit 2A Atcham Estate Shrewsbury Shropshire SY4 4UG Tel: 0743 761 889
DRIVING INSTRUCTORS' ASSOCIATION (DIAmond)	Safety House Beddington Farm Road Croydon Surrey CR0 4XZ Tel: 081 665 5151
DRIVING STANDARDS AGENCY	Stanley House Talbot Street Nottingham NG1 5GU Tel: 0602 474222
DVLA (Driver and Vehicle Licensing Agency)	Longview Road Morriston Swansea SA6 7JL Tel: 0792 782341 Driver enquiry unit: 0792 772 151 Vehicle enquiry unit: 0792 772 134
ENVIRONMENTAL TRANSPORT ASSOCIATION	The Old Post House Heath Road Weybridge

ADDRESS BOOK

Surrey KT13 8RS
Tel: 0932 828882

**THE GUILD OF EXPERIENCED
MOTORISTS**

Unit 1
Station Road
Forest Row
Sussex RH18 5EN
Tel: 0342 825676

**INSTITUTE OF ADVANCED
MOTORISTS**

IAM House
359–65 Chiswick High Road
London W4 4HS
Tel: 081 994 4403

**NATIONAL BREAKDOWN
RECOVERY CLUB**

PO Box 300
Leeds LS99 2LZ
Tel: 0532 393545

**NTDA (National Tyre
Distributors' Association)**

Suite B
1st floor
Elsinore House
Buckingham Street
Aylesbury HP20 2NQ
Tel: 0296 395933

RAC (Royal Automobile Club)

RAC House
M1 Cross
Brent Terrace
London NW2 1LT
Tel: 071 930 9142/3/4

**RETAIL MOTOR INDUSTRY
FEDERATION (trade association
of the retail motor industry)**

201 Gt Portland Street
London W1N 6AB
Tel: 071 580 9122

**RoSPA (Royal Society for
the Prevent of Accidents)**

Cannon House
The Priory
Queensway
Birmingham B4 6BS
Tel: 021 200 2461

SMMT (Society of Motor Manufacturers and Traders)

Forbes House
Halkin Street
London SW1X 7DS

TRADING STANDARDS OFFICE

See local telephone directory, under Borough or Council

Index